BEAR

HEART OF A HERO

THE STORY OF A MAN AND HIS GROUND ZERO
SEARCH AND RESCUE DOG

BY

CAPTAIN SCOTT SHIELDS

AND

NANCY M. WEST

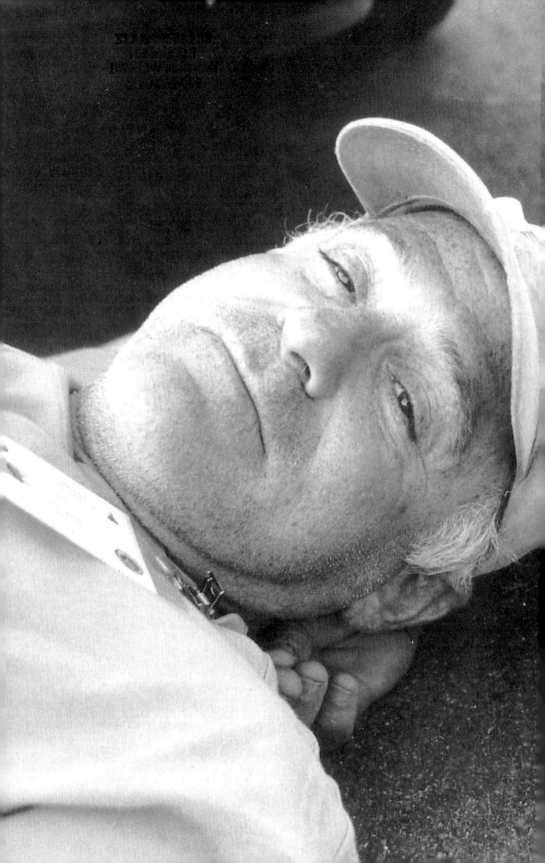

ISBN: 0-9743659-0-4

Hero Dog Publications
980 Broadway, P.O. Box 238
Thornwood, New York 10594

www.herodogpublications.com

Cover Photo, and photo spread (page (2–3): Jenny Warburg
Cover design and book layout: Jonathan Gullery, Budgetbookdesign.com

Printed in the United States of America

Hero Dog Publications is dedicated to publishing stories
about real service dogs and their human partners.

Fourth Printing

10 9 8 7 6 5

FOR ALL THE MEN, WOMEN, AND CANINES

WHO SERVE SO THAT OTHERS MAY LIVE

THE BEAR SEARCH AND RESCUE FOUNDATION
So That Others May Live
MISSION
To provide training, equipment, and transportation to search and rescue teams around the country

For more information contact: www.bearsearchandrescue.org
The Bear Search and Rescue Foundation a not-for-profit 501 C (3)
A copy of our annual report may be obtained, upon request, from The Bear Search and
Rescue Foundation or from the New York State Attorney General's Charities Bureau,
120 Broadway, New York, New York 10271

CONTENTS

GOODWILL AMBASSADOR

APPENDIX

FOREWORD

It was a Saturday afternoon in November of 2001, and I was at home doing research for a children's book about war dogs when I suddenly remembered that I had been assigned to chauffeur detail for my daughter's Girl Scout troop. It was my duty to retrieve six girls from the Westchester County Center in White Plains, New York, where they were doing community service work for the Annual International Cat Show. Being a harried suburban mom, I had expediency in the forefront of my mind. To this end, I had arranged for my daughter to meet me outside of the busy convention center at a specified time. I was running late. After circling the designated area for the better part of thirty minutes and finding no Girl Scouts, I paid the ten-dollar fee to park my car, an additional ten-dollar admission charge for the cat show, and stormed into the convention hall.

I combed through aisle after aisle of information tables, product exhibits, and cages filled with demure felines of every shape, color, and size until I finally caught sight of my daughter and her friends. I was almost within earshot when I tripped over a large golden retriever that was blocking my route. I was so startled to see a dog in the folds of cat culture that I blurted out, "Excuse me!"

The dog looked up at me with sagacious brown eyes as if to say, *What's your hurry, lady? If you don't slow down and sniff life as you go, you might miss something important!* His fur was reddish in color, the shade of an Irish setter, and he had a massive head and a muzzle that was whitened with age. He wore what appeared to be an orange service vest with badges sewn onto it, but without my eyeglasses I couldn't read the names and logos. I glanced around for his owner but he seemed to be on his own. Something about him intrigued me, and before I knew it I was following him up and down the cat aisles. I couldn't keep from smiling as I watched him methodically move from cage to cage, sniffing each one from top to bottom, as if reading an important document by nose. He never flinched from his task, and held his ground even when an irate occupant hissed and flashed claws in his face. Fascinated, I must have observed him for five or ten minutes when I heard a nearby man's voice call out, "Oso!" With that this canine interloper turned on a dime and loped off out of sight.

When I caught up with the golden retriever he was surrounded by admirers, including my Girl Scouts. A gentleman in a blue uniform with the words 'Marine Safety Service' stenciled across the back stepped forward and introduced himself as Captain Scott Shields, Bear's "dad." He said that he supervised water safety for events in and around New York harbor, and that he and Bear were at the show because Bear was receiving the cats' "Hero Dog of the Year Award" for his search and rescue work and efforts at Ground Zero.

Not only was I thrilled to meet one of the 9/11 dogs from the World Trade Center, but in the course of researching my book on war dogs I had also read up on these amazing search and rescue (SAR) canines. I was so excited to have the opportunity to learn more firsthand that I immediately began firing questions at his handler. "How did you train Bear?" was my first question.

"I raised my son on doctors Spock and Freud," responded Captain Shields with a smile.

It was a cute answer, but not what I had in mind. I knew that SAR dogs went through rigorous training to learn their trade. (I later learned that Bear had been trained in search and rescue techniques.) So I tried another question.

"Are you with FEMA (Federal Office of Emergency Management)

or another search and rescue organization?"

"No, I'm not really a dog guy," he smiled. "I'm trained in national disaster management."

Okay, I thought, I'm batting zero for two: one more try.

"Does Bear do obedience work? I'm sure he's earned his share of titles." This time it was my turn to smile, because it was easy to see that Bear was impeccably obedient.

With this question Captain Shields laughed and shook his head, "No, never. He grew up in Westport where there's no leash law. He learned most of what knows from his mother and working with me on the job." Feeling like I had struck out on gathering any insightful information on search and rescue dogs, I thanked him and turned to leave.

Yet something about this man and his dog had piqued my curiosity and I stayed at the periphery of the gathering crowd to watch the two of them.

Through my research I've read many accounts of the unique relationships that developed between canines and their military handlers during wartime. I've spoken with Vietnam Veterans who to this day weep over the loss of their four-legged partners from all those years ago. Many of these accounts and people describe situations where dogs exceeded the scope of their training to perform heroically beyond all expectations, and to save countless lives in the process.

As I continued to observe Captain Shields and Bear, my thoughts drifted back nearly four decades to the farm collie I grew up with in upstate New York. Shannon, who never knew the meaning of the word *leash*, was never trained according to any national or military standards. His *training* was by his own design and every bit *on the job*. When the neighbors' horses broke through their fencing Shannon took it upon himself to herd them back. He often retrieved my brother and me from neighbor's homes at the simple request of my mother.

Shannon was so punctual about meeting my four- o'clock school bus each day that we often joked that he wore a watch. But Shannon also engaged in other behavior that seemed to inch out of the realm of human explanation. When my father was going through a difficult illness Shannon began showing up at his office, a distance of five miles away. Once my father was out of danger, these mysterious visits stopped.

The more I watched Captain Shields and Bear interact, the more mesmerized I was by their relationship. It was easy to see the tremendous bond of love and respect that existed between them, but their *partnership* went far beyond this. Like a pair of dancers who are perfectly choreographed, they moved through space in complete awareness of each other's motions.

Over the course of the next year I spent many hours with Bear and Scott collecting notes for a children's book that I hoped to write about their life and adventures together. I traveled with them to events, videotaped their activities around New York, and interviewed countless people who had known them in their early days in Westport, Connecticut, as well as those who met them for the first time at Ground Zero. When Scott asked me to help him write a "biography" about Bear I was honored to assist him. Assembling the memories of a departed loved one is always difficult, especially when that loss is still being mourned.

Like the amazing accounts of comradeship told by Vietnam Veterans, Scott and Bear's story transcends the boundary of the *human-canine relationship*. In the almost thirteen years that Bear and Scott lived, worked, and played together something magical occurred. They learned to read the subtle nuances of each other's behavior and to intuit one another's thoughts. More than any other factor, it was this *magic* that enabled them to make their way and accomplish their work at *Ground Zero*.

Nancy M. West, April 2003

ACKNOWLEDGEMENTS

I am forever indebted to Bear's mother, Honey, who taught me to love something other than myself. And to my own mother who always set a right and honest example to live by.

My deepest thanks goes to my sister, Patty, whose unending support has allowed me to *serve others*.

My sincere thanks is also sent to my high school teacher, Arthur Abramowitz, at the Windsor Mountain School in Lenox, Massachusetts. He taught me how to analyze systems, and showed me that every system has a way around it.

I will always be appreciative of the National Inter-Agency Civil Military Institute that trained me to understand how to respond at a strategic and tactical level during a national disaster.

Finally, I wish to thank Bear as he was the best friend, partner, and *son* any man could hope to have....

S.S.

SPECIAL THANKS

A special thanks to Andrew Furber, Arthur Freed, PS 183, White Plains High School, and Diana Campbell for allowing us to print their wonderful tributes to Bear. Thank you also to Elizabeth Zack and Judy Freed for all of their assistance and advice.

S.S. and N.W.

A LETTER TO BEAR

Dear Bear,

On September 10, 2001, I took a flight from Los Angeles to Dusseldorf, Germany to begin a teaching assignment. I arrived in Dusseldorf on September 11th at noon Germany time.

Another American friend picked me up at the airport and we stopped to have coffee before proceeding onward. The coffee bar had a large, wide screen television. It was on, and all the people we saw there were transfixed by images of smoking destruction. I glanced at it and thought everyone was watching a Bruce Willis "Die Hard" movie or something. We sat down and ordered coffee.

While we were waiting for our coffee, we began to stare at the television screen and I gradually became aware that we were watching a live news broadcast of a horrible accident in New York City. It seemed as though a plane had veered off course and smashed into the World Trade Center. Then, as we were watching this broadcast, another plane could be seen heading for the second tower, and soon it, too, crashed into the second building.

We were both dumbstruck! How could this happen and what was the meaning of this? Then, as we stared uncomprehendingly at the screen, one of the towers collapsed. Shortly after the second one did too. We looked at each other and began to cry….

As the weeks followed days, we kept abreast of what was happening by tuning into CNN on the television and reading the CNN news on the Internet. The horror was simply too big to absorb and so overwhelming that I found I couldn't watch it over and over.

But one picture on CNN encapsulated the incredible sorrow I was feeling. It gave me a smaller piece of the tragedy to focus on, enabling me to come to terms with the reality of the incomprehensible.

It was a photo of a dog—an aged, exhausted-looking golden retriever rescue dog named Bear, and I began to follow your story.

Following you helped me to deal with what happened by focusing my attention on one small part of a horrific and unbelievable disaster. I couldn't absorb the big picture—it was simply too much. So I think it's accurate to say that you led me out of my anger, despair, and confusion by showing me the beauty that comes from tragedy: the selfless giving to help others.

One thing of beauty that comes from horror is that all involved have the opportunity to show the rest of us what humanity is really made of: love, caring, and willingness to give without personal gain. Though I couldn't watch the workers and the people left behind when their friends and relatives died in the disaster, I could watch you: selflessly and tirelessly showing the world that when disaster strikes, there's work to do.

You as a dog…as man's best friend…show us how we can all be when the going gets tough. You're gone now, Bear, but your memory and work live on. I can't thank you enough for what you gave me.

Diana Campbell 2003

INTRODUCTION

I had always been a student of history, and I believed most of what I read in history books. As I grew older I realized that even the most accurate writers and interpreters of history often get it wrong.

Bear was a kind of "poster dog" for Ground Zero. His story and image came to signify the work of all of the search and rescue canines for many people who read about him, saw him on television, or met him on the streets of New York City. Both the media and people we met repeatedly asked me for details of Bear's life and our work at the World Trade Center. These requests and my need to set the facts of history straight became the impetus for writing this book.

The fraternity of the thousand-meter stare was one I always wanted to earn the right to join. In retrospect I guess this was just some boyish flight of fancy. *Be careful of what you wish for, the saying goes.* Now, being able to see this look in another's eyes, recognizing an unspoken brotherhood as I pass another on the street, and acknowledging its tragic consequences for so many people, makes me realize that this kind of fraternity serves as a turning point in life. After working at Ground Zero, I'll never look at life from the same vantage point again.

As I come to the end of these words and spaces on paper I realize that after all is said and done, I'd like to be remembered most as Bear's and Honey's "dad."

Scott Shields, June 2003

REMEMBERING . . .

It was one more somber call for the firefighters of New York City. With lights flashing and sirens respectfully silenced, a convoy of gleaming rigs and emergency vehicles solemnly turned onto the FDR Drive and headed north out of Manhattan. But unlike the countless funeral details the firefighters had led in the twelve months since the World Trade Center tragedy this one had a different destination for a different kind of hero. Along with a small group of close friends, I rode with the New York Aviation Volunteer Fire Department, Engine Company 3, to the Hartsdale Pet Cemetery in Hartsdale, New York.

I sat alone in a jump seat of the lead rig. Stowed away in the back of the engine, in a plain cardboard carton inscribed "Bear" were the remains of my partner and companion of nearly thirteen years. We were on what I thought was our last mission together. As I watched the New York skyline melt away in the warm September haze, the memories of our years together came tumbling back to me....

"Give us Bear!" "Where's Bubba?" "Get us the golden!" "Bring us the dog!" Over and over again, throughout the afternoon and into the first grisly night of September 11th, 2001, firemen desperately shouted out for Bear's help. These guys had only one golden retriever with whom to search acres of smoldering rubble, and they couldn't get enough of Bear. Without man's best friend, finding the hidden and buried victims of one of the greatest tragedies in the history of America was like trying to find needles in a haystack. What had begun as a small team of rescuers following me and Bear had grown to hundreds of men by nightfall. All of them were depending on one dog's nose.

Bear, ash-caked and exhausted, wove through the mosaics of mangled steel and crushed concrete. He sensed the urgency and resolute actions of the rescuers who followed his every move. He never faltered, never stopped, but continued at a deliberate pace, alerting each time he made a find or "hit." Sometimes the men lifted him onto girders too precarious for a grown man's weight to withstand. Other times he was lowered into crevices or voids to nose into spots too small or deemed too dangerous for a human rescuer. Many of the voids were filled with steam, which meant that Bear was working blind. We'd lose sight of him and I'd think, *oh my God, he's gone. I'll never see my baby again.* Then he'd reappear with this look in his eyes that said, *I'm okay, dad. Where do you want me to go next?* He understood that we had journeyed into harm's way, but he had a mission to perform.

So many times I was certain that Bear would asphyxiate from the dust he inhaled. Thick gray soot filled his ears, oozed out of his eyes, and packed his nostrils. I stopped every hour to wash them all out, but it was a losing battle. Sometimes we had to dodge pieces of debris that were blowing off the pile or from the partially demolished buildings. I felt so guilty that I had a helmet and he had nothing to protect him. It was a small miracle that he was never hit.

By the end of that first night Bear's paws were flaming red with irritation. Bear never wore boots; he had never trained in them, and I was afraid here, in this place of utter destruction, they might throw off his balance and he'd fall into one of the voids and perish. But now the pulverized cement and glass we had to work in wedged between his pads. Many times Bear and I got to the point where we were both too tired to stand. Panting, Bear would slosh down on his belly in ponds of putrid water and try to drink it. The water that was being pumped from fireboats that had anchored at North Cove, the marina closest to the World Trade Center, to quell the fires was filled with ash, debris, and other toxins, including human waste.

We were moving along a beam one time when a piece of twisted metal gouged Bear's back. It was a deep puncture wound but Bear kept working. He always had a high tolerance for pain.

Time and again Bear would stop and burrow his head into a foot of ash. Sometimes the ash was still warm, and I worried that he would nose into a hot piece of debris and get burned. Then Bear's body would go rigid and his right paw would scratch at the ground. The men would quickly remove any large pieces of rubble by hand and then dig with picks and shovels to unearth Bear's find. We never waited but moved on to the next spot. When I heard the shout for a "body bag" I always knew that Bear had been right. The chilling words would toll out across the debris field. A hushed silence always followed. It was a silence so vast that you could hardly breathe.

Since our first days at Ground Zero people—often complete strangers I meet on the street—have asked me, *how many victims did Bear find?* I understand human curiosity, especially around a national tragedy such as this one, but I've never been comfortable answering what has always struck me as a very sad question. My response to news reporters and others has always been, "too many...."

We worked through most of that first night. Firemen told me that Bear was the only rescue dog they saw working *the pile*, the term we used to describe the debris field of rubble known as Ground Zero, for the first six or seven hours. The strange thing is.... I never answered the 9/11 call for help as a search and rescue canine guy. I went to Ground Zero because I'm trained in emergency and national disaster management. Although Bear had some experience in search and rescue work he was only with me on the morning of September 11th because Bear was always at my side. *Bear was only with me because he was always at my side...*

I.

THE EARLY YEARS

"Dogs are not our whole life, but they make our lives whole."
Roger Caras

VOL. 26, NO 88 (USPS 857-040)   WESTPORT, CONNECTICUT   FRIDAY, NOVEMBER 3, 1989

A honey of a mommy

It could only happen on the Golden Half Mile.
Honey, the golden retriever mascot of the Susan Shields dress shop, became the mother of 11 puppies on Wednesday. The happy event took place in the store.
Meanwhile, Honey and her nine surviving pups are doing fine — in the Main Street office of the store's owner, Scott Shields.   *Photo by Rick D'Elia*

Bear's birth recorded for history in the Westport News.

Honey's first morning at home. I never could have guessed how this puppy would one day change my life and, through Bear, the lives of so many others. Honey's favorite toys were Disney characters. Mickey and Minnie were always her Favorites. What would Doctor Freud say? (Scott Shields)

HONEY

I never wanted a dog.

People always give me a sly smile when I say this but it's the truth. It wasn't that I didn't like dogs…I just never wanted the responsibility of having one! The woman I had been living with always begged for a puppy at Christmas. Each year I resisted, warning her about the pitfalls of pet ownership. She promised that she would take full responsibility for feeding and walking the dog, and for picking up the poop. So one December, I found myself standing in a pet shop in the mall in Trumbull, Connecticut, cradling an eight-week-old ball of golden fluff in my arms.

My girlfriend quickly lost interest in raising a dog. And by Valentine's Day, when she and I were history, I'd fallen head-over-paws in love with Honey, Bear's mom.

Honey was a soft-faced, wheat-colored golden retriever. I always liked to say she was half mule and all woman. She could be the most wonderful companion on this earth or she could be very, very stubborn. If Honey chose not to do something there was no amount of pleading, cajoling, or treat bribing that could make her budge. Before I got Honey I'd always been a freewheeling, independent-kind-of-guy with only myself to watch out for. Honey taught me how to put another life first. She was the love of my life, and for the next thirteen years she was my best friend and companion.

My first career was not in emergency management. My family had a dress design and manufacturing business with stores in Miami Beach and New York City. After graduating from Drew University in Madison, New Jersey, with a major in political science and art, and spending a year in Washington, D.C. as a researcher for a congressional committee, I had decided to move back to New York and enter the family business. I felt that my personality was better suited to an entrepreneurial style than that of a politician. It wasn't long before I had my own dress design and manufacturing company. I opened stores in Greenwich and Westport, Connecticut. My home store was in the charming shore town of Westport. Honey was a popular dog in this community, and when word got out that she was expecting I couldn't step foot outside my store without being asked, "When are the puppies due?" or "Have the puppies arrived yet?"

On November 1, 1989, I was driving to work with Honey in her usual spot beside me in the passenger seat. I reached my hand over toward her and felt a pool of warm liquid. My first thought was that my coffee had spilled, but when I checked I found that it was securely in place. That's when it hit me: Honey's water had broken. Like an expectant father I nearly panicked. I parked my car in the lot behind my store and ran to unlock the back entrance. I was so nervous and excited that I didn't see Honey slip in behind me. When I turned to call her inside she was nowhere to be found. Then I really did panic! "Honey!" I yelled out, but she was gone.

For weeks Honey had been constructing a kind of beaver's den with a roof made out of twigs and branches near the side of my garage. My friends and I had quite a chuckle out of watching her build this "nest" for her expectant family. Now the frightening thought crossed my mind that she might have tried to travel the two miles back to our home. I quickly ran around the building to see if she was waiting for me by the front entrance to the store. I unlocked the door and glanced into my office that was adjacent to the entryway. Honey was lying under my desk, and the birthing process had begun! Bear and his ten littermates came into the world under the desk in my office without a hitch.

When the *Westport News*, our local paper, heard that Honey's puppies had arrived, they rushed a photographer over to record the much-anticipated event. The proud mother and her puppies appeared on the cover of the next issue with the banner "A Honey of a Mommy." At the time, the editor said the cover produced more mail than any other cover story he'd ever done. These letters were both positive and negative. Most people said it was their favorite front page ever. Others said that I was wrong to allow my dog to have babies, and the *Westport News* irresponsible to feature the event! It often amazes me now that even Bear's humble birth was recorded for posterity.

In order to keep Honey and her brood with me while I worked, I kept cardboard cartons and playpens in all my stores. Customers loved playing with the roly-poly pups, and the pups were soon a major attraction in town. It was terrific training for the puppies because they quickly learned to socialize with strangers and exercise good manners. Besides, I never allowed them to get "nosey" with customers or leave paw-prints on costly evening gowns!

Of course, though, even the best-behaved dog will slip-up occasionally. I vividly recall the day my friend Jo Shields (no relation) poked her head into my office and asked if I was aware that Bear was sitting in my store's display window chewing on a hat that she said cost more than her weekly salary. A small crowd of window shoppers had stopped to enjoy his puppy capers. I was hissed and booed by the audience when I promptly put an end to Bear's shenanigans.

Bear and his littermates went to work with me every day.
(Scott Shields)

HONEY'S BEAR

It's difficult for me to think about this after all of our years together, but I never intended to keep Bear. He was the biggest and toughest of Honey's brood. I wasn't a "dog breeder" by any stretch of the imagination, so it never occurred to me that size was a positive attribute to have in a dog. Not only did I think he was a bit of a bully for regularly pushing his brothers and sisters away from Honey's milk, but I planned to keep the runt of the litter, the pup everyone called "Baby-Baby." I've always had a soft spot in my heart for the underdog.

Yet back then there was a little girl who came to the office everyday for seven weeks to play and care for the puppies. She walked, fed, and bathed them. She even cleaned up their poop...all without knowing that her parents planned to surprise her with one of the puppies, Bear. It was easy to find good homes for all of Honey's babies, and by the eighth week everyone had come by to pick up their pup. Only the runt and Bear were left. When the little girl showed up I placed Bear in her arms and she started to leave. But when she got to the vestibule she turned, looked up at me with enormous steel-blue eyes, and said, "I really wanted Baby-Baby." She had been such a great kid and so devoted to the puppies that I couldn't resist handing her the one I'd set my heart on. I took Bear out of her arms...and the rest is history. Just goes to show it sometimes pays to be a nice guy.

I always tell people that Bear was raised according to doctors Spock and Freud. In truth, half of what Bear knew he learned from his mom. She was forever his canine role model, and what he didn't learn from me he learned from her. Honey had a kind heart and loved children as well as all kinds of animals. Like the lioness that instructs her cubs in how to survive in the wilderness, Honey was Bear's best teacher. She showed him how to stop and observe traffic at intersections, and how to walk on narrow beams and planks when boarding boats. Given a choice between eating sirloin or chuck, Honey always would choose the more expensive cut of beef. I'll never know if Bear learned this at his Mom's knee or not, but until the day he died, Bear too always chose the better grade of beef. When he was still a puppy, I had trained Bear to never accept food from strangers. This was a practice Bear maintained until the first night at Ground Zero, when he ate ten steak sandwiches from a Salvation Army volunteer. It took eleven years and an act of war for Bear to break the habit of not accepting food from strangers.

Honey even taught me many lessons. On the few occasions when Bear annoyed her with his puppy antics she would push him onto his back and give a low growl on his neck to convey her disapproval. When I recommend this correction technique to friends with young dogs they often smirk at my method. Then they come back later and tell me it works like a charm!

Honey and Bear also had their unique differences. Honey always gave me an affirmative response to questions by wagging her tail. One day, Bear walked into the living room while I was watching television and quickly glanced from me to the door. This time when I asked if he wanted to go "out," I noticed that he raised his ears ever so slightly. I let him out, and he immediately did his business. I'll never know how long he had been trying to communicate with me in this manner—I had missed his cues because I thought they'd be the same as his mom's! But for whatever reason, I was observant at that moment, and we rarely misunderstood each other again. This flinching of his ears became Bear's way of giving me the affirmative for just about everything.

Sitting on the store couch at holiday time with "the family."
Honey was so proud of her babies!
(Scott Shields)

Mother and son playing with Bear's first teddy bear.
(Scott Shields)

Mother and son practicing their tracking techniques.
(Scott Shields)

Even as a puppy people told me how much
Bear reminded them of a noble lion.
(Scott Shields)

Honey and Bear as Queen and King of the "snowball."
(Scott Shields)

Bear loved to swim with the swans and ducks but never
chased them. He tracked and rescued injured animals including waterfowl.
People often called me to have Bear find their lost cats Bear loved cats!
(Scott Shields)

Bear at an island cleanup when I was warden of
Cockenoe Island in Long Island Sound.

An example of Bear handling the lines of my boat.
Westport's Long Shore Country Club is in the background.
(Nancy Meusse)

This is how we spent our days in the spring, summer, and
even early fall on our island in Long Island Sound. I always
wanted human kids but never had them. Honey and Bear
turned out to be the best "kids" any man could ever hope to
have. (Scott Shields)

A typical day out on the boat with Honey and Bear.
(Scott Shields)

The stream bed in Winslow Park (known to old residents as
"the Baron's") was a favorite spot for all seasons.
(Scott Shields)

Bear was raised in Westport where there's no leash law, only what's called a responsibility law. As a result, he spent nearly twelve years acting independently in a variety of environments: congested city streets, forests, open beaches, and bustling marinas. Both Honey and Bear often accompanied me to New York City where they rarely wore a leash—except when requested to by local authorities. They were comfortable maneuvering and taking direction "off leash" even in the heaviest trafficked areas. It was simply a part of their daily lives, and it was what allowed Bear to make the transition to the chaotic and stressful environment at Ground Zero without so much as skipping a beat.

I tried to give Bear plenty of structured training time too when he was a puppy. Much of this "formal" training took place in Westport's Winslow Park, a thirty-acre nature preserve smack in the center of this wonderful community. Bear was happiest working out of doors, and there were just enough diversions in the park to challenge his canine instinct. The meadows and woodlands enabled us to work on directional commands at greater and greater distances. Often I would enlist the help of a friend to join us. Initially, we sat about ten yards apart, and took turns calling Bear to come. His reward was freeze-dried liver, a treat I only use when training. Bear was a quick learner, so it wasn't long before we added the "sit," "down," "turn around," "go left," "go right," "stop," "go back," and all of the other commands that made him a joy as a partner.

Workers on the pile often commented on Bear's steadfast attitude and self-confidence on the job. While his formal training was important, I'll always believe that it was Connecticut's liberal leash laws, and ultimately his life of "responsibility" in Westport, that made him the dog he was at Ground Zero.

As Bear progressed in his training we broadened our horizons to obstacle courses. Westport's Compo Beach has an enormous wooden playground that was constructed by hundreds of community volunteers. There are slides, ladders, moving carousels, tunnels, large moving platforms (to practice maneuvers on unstable ground), and high beams to challenge even the most ambitious puppy. In the off-season dogs were welcome without leashes. Honey had already mastered clambering over moving platforms and walking adroitly on narrow beams, and always set a good example for her son. Whenever Bear and his mom performed on a piece of equipment there would be cheers and applause from park visitors. There's nothing like lavish praise to make a golden kid catch on fast!

I've always been somewhat unorthodox in my dog training methods and this has extended to the command language I use as well. Although German is the foreign language most frequently used (for example, it's used in Schutzhund training, a sport that evaluates a dog's ability at tracking, obedience, and protection work), I'd trained Honey in English and French. When the time came to teach Bear, however, I decided to train him in Spanish and English. Having their own individual language made it easier for Honey and Bear to distinguish whom I was speaking to when we were working, training, or simply out for a day of fun. Later, when Bear and I worked in marinas near Hispanic neighborhoods his bilingual ability was useful for another reason. Bear was a large dog and children were often afraid of him. When they realized that he spoke their native language he was immediately accepted and always became a big hit. His reputation as the "Oso" (the "Bear") grew.

I trained Bear to wait for me for long periods of time, even hours, on busy city sidewalks while I worked or went into grocery stores and restaurants. People always asked me how I had done this. The first part of my answer was that I had trained him in Westport, where I felt secure that he would be "safe." I never worried about Bear's well-being on the sidewalks of this cozy town. All of the shop-keepers and many of the pedestrians knew him by name. The second part of my answer was that I had Bear "wait" for something he really wanted. I began by having him stay for short stretches of time outside a local grocery store while I went to buy his "cookies" (which for Bear usually meant roast beef—his favorite food). Gradually, he learned to wait patiently for longer and longer periods. Even when our friends tried to lure Bear away from his assigned post he would not budge. He was simply waiting for his "dad."

There's nothing more pleasurable than teaching a dog to work at what he does best. As every one knows, goldens love to retrieve. So I had Bear first learn this skill by retrieving his lunch. Nearly every day at noontime Honey and Bear and I would visit "Oscar's," Westport's famous deli. I always ordered a pound of roast beef and had it split into two bags. Honey and Bear would each carry their "doggie bag" back to work or the park. (It was Lee Papageorge, the owner of Oscar's, who had run to the Westport News to inform them that Honey had given birth.) Bear's other favorite item to carry was my hat (he loved to jump up and steal it off my head!), and during our days at Ground Zero he enjoyed carrying my hardhat for me. It put a lot of smiles on the grim faces of the rescue workers, and I think it gave Bear an anchor in that sea of tragedy.

Bear and Honey's favorite activity was swimming. Initially I trained them in my swimming pool. Once they had mastered their strokes, I put harnesses on them and took them to Cockenoe Island, just off the coast from Westport. The island is one of the most popular spots for boaters in Long Island Sound. For years I volunteered on the Cockenoe Island Conservation Commission. There were always kids in the water, and I wanted Honey and Bear to get used to swimming around people. It soon became a weekend ritual for the kids to "ride the water doggies." Bear and Honey were happiest when they had a child on each side holding their harnesses, and another holding on to their tail. Watching my "sea dogs" swim with the kids always reminded me of the "swim-with-the-dolphins" attraction that's so popular at Sea World.

My involvement out on the island led to my volunteering with many other environmental marine groups over the next few years. Foremost amongst these was doing water quality studies for the Long Island Sound Task Force and water-sampling work for "Save the Sound," a successful grassroots ecological organization. Honey and Bear and I spent many hours visiting the small islands and tidal marshes in Long Island Sound.

I trained Bear and Honey to track poachers and not pursue nesting birds or other small animals. Watching Bear gently carry injured birds back to me in his powerful jaws often brought tears to my eyes. I think that this was one of the jobs Bear loved most. We would then take the birds to a local nature center. Eventually, both Bear and Honey were named members of the Cockenoe Island Commission. To my knowledge, they are the only two animals ever appointed to a Connecticut Commission!

When Bear was about five years old I decided to make a complete career and life-style change. Although I loved the fashion business and was financially successful at it, I was a child of the sixties. I had always hoped that I could, in some small way, make a difference in this world. I gradually began taking emergency management courses and before long I was hooked on the field. As Frances Edwards-Winslow, Director of the Office of Emergency Services for San Jose, California, stated in a lecture to federal emergency management directors, "Those seeking a career in emergency management must be more interested in doing good than in doing well. The rewards are internal and personal, but seldom material." I was flattered when Dr. Edwards-Winslow then cited me and explained that a diverse professional background coupled with a liberal arts degree could prove to be a great preparation for a career in emergency management.

Both emergency management, including national disaster response, and marine work (keeping people safe during boating and swimming events), had always been special interests of mine. It seemed natural to meld them together, and so I started a marine safety consulting business. Over the years I worked my way up to Safety Officer for many of the major water events in New York Harbor.

Through my marine safety work, Honey and Bear spent hours on vessels of all shapes and sizes. As retrievers they were extremely useful. Bear's great strength enabled him to assist me with docking my boat and handling the lines. He began this part of his training by retrieving a rubber cong toy with a heavy rope looped through it that was knotted at both ends. I taught him to "pick up the line," "go back," "drop it," and so forth. I also encouraged him to play tug-of-war with it. Eventually, I tied the cong to one of my boat lines (I owned a Center Console Aquasport, which was the perfect size boat for Bear to work), and instructed him to jump in the water and carry the toy that was tied to the line to shore. Before long Bear had learned to tug the boat's anchor line and pull the craft to the beach.

Even though I knew Bear was a strong dog, it always amazed me when he hauled the vessel in to shore. To perfect this process I eventually put a bungee cord on the anchor line off the stern. Along with this stern anchor, I put a regular anchor off the bow. When I dropped both anchors Bear would haul the one line into land. I could then let out as much line as I wanted, while instructing him to move up the beach. After Bear pulled the boat to shore we could disembark. I would then instruct him to "drop" the line, and the bungee would pull the boat out into deeper water so that the boat would not ground when the tide went out. Folks would line up on the beach to watch the "big golden" perform, and visitors aboard the boat were always relieved they didn't have to wade in to shore.

People often ask me if Bear worked the way he did at Ground Zero as a result of training or instinct. I tell them it was a subtle interplay of both. Bear was trained in a variety of environments that mimicked to a greater or lesser degree the debris pile at the World

Trade Center. In truth, the fabricated training environments on which we had all practiced couldn't compare with the magnitude of devastation the dogs there actually faced. Not only were the 16 acres of rubble (they felt like a thousand acres) impossible to duplicate, but the stressful working conditions were unimaginable and therefore impossible to simulate. On the site, Bear was endowed with energy, strength, stamina, and a persistence of will. He also was blessed with a magnificent nose. But beyond these factors, his innate pattern of behaviors (or instinct) was so fully developed and fine-tuned that he was able to gracefully and confidently perform his job. Training is always important, but if it's not coupled with innate abilities and good instinct then we would never get the desired results. To put it another way—we're only as good as our dog's instinct and nose.

II.

WORLD TRADE CENTER DISASTER

"A dog doesn't know enough to be anything but a hero."
Albert Payson Terhune, <u>Bruce</u>

MAP OF LOWER MANHATTAN

USS Intrepid

↑ **West Side Highway**

Hudson River

West Street

10.

← **Chambers Street**

8.,9.

Vesey Street

4.   **11.**

1.

12. → **5.**   **2.**

7.

3.

6.

NEW YORK HARBOR

Battery

Brooklyn →

N

W ← → E

S

KEY
1. 1 World Trade Center (North Building)
2. 2 World Trade Center (South Building)
3. Marriott Hotel
4. 3 World Financial Center(AMEX)
5. 2 World Financial Center
6. 1 World Financial Center
7. North Cove
8. Rockefeller Park
9. Stuyvesant High School
10. Pier 25
11. U.S. Custom
12. Winter Garden

[46]

GOING IN

On Tuesday, September 11, 2001, I was sharing a house with my sister, Patty, on the last road in Greenwich, Connecticut, before you get to Westchester County, New York. I had moved there from Westport after a divorce to be closer to my work in and around New York City.

Although I had grown up in both Miami Beach and Manhattan, I had lived in southern Connecticut shore towns for nearly half my life. Many men and women in these Connecticut towns commute daily into Manhattan, but the mere 35 miles between The World Trade Towers and Greenwich might just as well be 1000, given the difference in their landscapes! The 110-story North and South Towers of the World Trade Center soared out of a sea of impressive concrete and steel skyscrapers. This was a far cry from the protected woodlands, beaches, fields, and streams of Greenwich.

The morning started as it had for nearly eleven years. I was in a pretty deep snooze when I suddenly felt two dark eyes staring at me over the horizon of my blankets. Bear had penetrating soulful eyes and a steadfast gaze that was inescapable. He jumped onto the bed. "What's the hurry, Face-man?" I said, giving his belly a good rubbing. Over the years I had come up with a lot of nicknames for Bear. This one came about because strangers often stopped us on the street to say he was the most handsome dog they'd ever seen, and "Face-man" is what the handsome character on the 1980's television series "The A-Team" was called.

Bear's good looks were also responsible for my meeting my ex-wife. I was walking on the beach in Westport with Honey and Bear when a woman walked up to me and said, "Do you want to have babies?" Naturally I gave her an ear-to-ear smile. "Wipe that grin off your face," she said. "I don't mean with me. I mean your dog. He's the most handsome golden retriever I've ever seen, and I'd love to breed him with my female golden." And that's how Bear eventually became a "dad."

When we went outside for Bear to make his morning rounds, I remember looking at the sun rising to the east in a flawless pale blue sky, and thinking it would be a perfect day to fly. Years ago I had obtained a pilot's license, and days offering seemingly endless visibility continued to tantalize and entice my imagination. Little did I know that within hours this thought about flying high above would leave me with a queasy feeling.

I watched Bear make his morning rounds. He carefully perused the yard for signs that interlopers might have passed through the night before. When he had satisfied his curiosity he stood by my car to let me know that he was ready for the next step in our morning ritual, a visit to a local park. As usual, I lowered the front passenger window on my Chevy Nova, while Bear coiled his body into position. "Oso, arriba!" I instructed, pointing, and Bear gracefully leapt through the car's open window and settled down in his seat.

We drove to one of our favorite local haunts, Byram Shore Park. It's on the water and is a picture-perfect New England harbor with jutting cliffs and rocky islands. What's more, it's a great place to watch the day unfold. Sometimes we stopped to chat with the harbormaster, Bob Crawford, a friendly, jovial man and a dead ringer for Santa Claus. I used to love to tell the kids we met at Byram Shore that Santa spent the summer at Byram Beach. We didn't see Bob in his office though, so we strolled along the dock looking at the anchored boats and dramatic waterfront homes.

My precious Honey had passed away two months earlier and each day had become a struggle without her. Friends often told me that I put all of the love I might have had for human kids into my love for Honey and Bear. My friends were probably right. Honey was my "first child" and there will never be another one like her in my eyes. I was certain that Bear felt the same aching loneliness I felt without her, and I was adamant that we both got plenty of social time with other dogs in the park. Bear was especially fond of large females (Newfoundlands and Saint Bernards were two favorite breeds), and he usually "fell in love" at first sight. To put it another way, at the ripe old age of eleven, Bear still loved chasing girls. Unfortunately, this particular morning presented no infatuations for Bear.

Once we finished making all the necessary stops, we paid our respects at the statue of Yogi, a national police hero dog of the year, who is honored in the park. Yogi was a friend of Bear's, and a favorite boyfriend of Honey's. I had made it my habit to clean the area around the memorial, picking up any broken beer bottles or cigarette stubs that I found littered there. A few times a year I placed flowers or a wreath beneath the statue. Bear and I always placed dog biscuits at the base of the monument too. We did this so Yogi and Honey would know we had been there and remembered them. This might sound silly, but I always leave an odd number of biscuits. The extra one is for Honey, since she had an enormous sweet tooth. When our work was done, Bear and I headed for home. Little did I know as I watched him prancing alongside of me that our halcyon days would soon be over....

• • •

I was at the breakfast table in the kitchen, watching television when ABC News made the announcement.

"What could make a plane hit the tallest building in New York on a beautiful day like this?" my sister, Patty, asked.

I went through a short inventory of reasons in my mind, trying to stay conservative in my permutations of possibilities. "Probably a novice pilot getting in too close in an effort to show off," I said. I consciously tried to push the thought of terrorism out of my mind. I didn't want to assume, as so many had with the Oklahoma City bombing, that foreign terrorists were responsible.

Ordinarily, as a marine safety officer, I would never respond to an incident of this type unless I was called, but somewhere between telling myself it was a tragic accident and watching the news, I decided to drive to Manhattan. The truth is that both my background in national disaster preparedness and my gut told me this was no accident.

"You're not really going to New York?" Patty said incredulously when I told her I was leaving. "They'll have plenty of people there to handle it. Besides, you'll never be allowed anywhere near the Trade Center," she added.

Patty nearly convinced me she was right. While she tried to talk some sense into me, I tried calling my contacts at the Red Cross, the Federal Office of Emergency Management (FEMA), and the New York City Parks Police Department. All the lines were busy.

We were still talking when a newscaster announced that the second tower had been hit. For a moment, Patty and I looked at each other in disbelief. Then I turned to Bear who, throughout the debate with my sister, had been patiently waiting for me by the door. In an instant I realized it was the right decision to go; Bear had sensed what was in my heart before I did.

Just before we left, I put Bear's Red Cross ID collar around his neck. He had received it when demonstrating search and rescue procedures at the Red Cross "Stand Tall Camp" for kids the summer before. I knew we were going into a rough situation, and I wanted him tagged just in case we were separated. When I looked at him wearing the international insignia of relief for victims of war and disaster, I got a strange feeling in the pit of my stomach. That's when it hit me hard. This was the real thing: a national event of historic proportions. Our lives would never be the same again.

"Okay, Bubba," I said once we were in the car. Along with "Oso" this was a favorite nickname I had for him whenever we were working. Then I repeated a motto I live by when things go wrong, "Improvise, Adapt, Overcome." Bear always sat in the front seat next to me, and now he turned and gave me one of his wise-old-sage looks. I knew that he understood. He could read the tenseness in my body and had closely watched me gather the disaster equipment we would need. He knew we were on a mission.

The drive from King Street in the northwest corner of Greenwich to the corner of West and Chambers, a drive that can easily take up to ninety minutes on a normal Tuesday morning, took just 38 minutes, a record for us. The closer we got to the city the fewer cars we saw. All we started spotting were more volunteers, with flashing lights like ours, as well as official emergency vehicles. I remember being struck by the fact that so many were responding to the news so rapidly from what I presumed was Westchester County and western Connecticut. I never guessed that volunteers would not only respond from the far reaches of our tri-state area (New York, New Jersey, and Connecticut), but from across the United States and around the world within a day's time. In fact, within only a few hours I would find myself assisting a helicopter crew from Fox Flight Air Ambulance of Canada.

I had consciously made a decision not to look at the speedometer as we drove to the site of the emergency. My adrenaline was pumping, but after one harrowing turn on what could have been only two tires, Bear looked at me as if to say: *Don't forget the first rule in emergency management, Dad, 'Never jeopardize your own life.'* Before the morning was over Bear and I would abandon this caveat, but right then, sensing Bear's concern and having scared even myself, I eased off the accelerator.

The search and rescue group I led in from Massachusetts.
We were preparing to go back onto the pile.
(l. to r. is Michael Goldberg and Jactive, rescuer whose name I have lost,
me and Bear, and Frederick Golba with Ammo.) (Scott Shields)

Scott, Bear and a Battalion Chief
take a break at Ground Zero

Bear and I stopped for a water break. We were
immediately surrounded by the world's press.
(Scott Shields)

Field-expedient rest: that's the technical term.
In other words, working eighteen-hour days, we caught "forty-winks"
wherever we could. (Jenny Warburg)

Bear and I on a Coast Guard shuttle operation headed
north away from Ground Zero.

Ground Zero from New York Harbor
immediately after the first tower collapsed.
(Stan Tankursley)

The leaning façade that came to
represent Ground Zero to the world.
(Tom Fletcher)

Crushed vehicles along West Street.
(Tom Fletcher)

When we reached the Henry Hudson Bridge, the only tollbooth on the trip, all emergency vehicles were being waved through, and we were permitted to pass. As we crossed over the convergence of the Hudson and Harlem Rivers, I thought about some of the marine rescues we had been involved with in the treacherous waters below known as the "Spuyten Duyvil," (spit of the devil). Kayaks were often caught in the rivers' convergence, where currents create rip-tide conditions, making rescues hazardous. Little did I realize that going through the toll was just the first of many devil's gates we would pass through that day. I also recall looking out over the bridge and seeing Columbia University's boathouse sitting peacefully near the water. It was rapidly dawning on me that we were at war, and I wondered when any of us might be able to enjoy recreational activities on the water again.

With these thoughts in mind, I needed to calm my nerves. The best method for me to do this has always been to think in hard, practical terms. I began to mentally review my training in national disaster management. Although my daily work has been in marine safety, I've completed a multitude of FEMA, Red Cross, Coast Guard, and National Guard courses over the years (the later taught through the National Inter-agency Civil-Military Institute (NICI)). Among other things, the NICI trains emergency management professionals to work with a multitude of agencies in major events or during times of national crises. These can be natural disasters or man-made events from hurricanes and earthquakes to acts of terrorism. One of the most important lessons taught by NICI is to think in terms of an overall strategy to a crisis, rather than just isolated tactics.

Being able to bring together diverse groups to maximize a response to any form of disaster is critical to its success. Taken to its core, disaster management is simply event management magnified; all lessons learned in one situation are applicable to the other. For example, knowing how and what is needed for a safe swimming event in New York Harbor or an outdoor concert for a hundred thousand people in New York's Central Park can acquaint us with and teach us about lessons for disasters of national proportions.

To this end, I immediately turned my attention to visualizing the World Trade Center area. Manhattan, as most folks know, is an island, and the Trade Towers sit perched on its lower west side where the land tapers off. This means that only a couple of roads access the site from the north where most of the emergency vehicles would originate. Given the magnitude of the disaster, I knew this would lead to infamous New York City gridlock. Also, because Manhattan is an island, and because I often work in and around New York Harbor, I realized the water would play a key role. I just wasn't certain of where or how it would be important yet.

I thought about a host of other things as I drove. I considered what I knew about the capabilities of our federal, state, and local authorities, and about how these organizations should interact and communicate with each other and the military during a disaster. Such a coordination of services had never been tested in the Northeast before—especially during a national crisis. I reflected on the courses I had taken in dealing with hazardous materials and the response to chemical weapons, something we all feared might have been deployed at the time. I thought about what specific contaminates we might have to deal with. I considered the stability of the site itself, and like the rest of the country, I worried about when and where there might be another attack. I wondered if the next strike would be again directed at New York City. Finally, I reminded myself of one of the most important lessons NICI had taught me: how to know when *not* to go by the book.

I also mentally reviewed my own individual preparedness, including the items I had packed in my car. As was my habit, I reviewed the list with Bear: "We've got repelling lines, medical kit, thermal blankets, tool kit, oxygen bottle, power drills, pry bars, beam lights (million candle lights), GPS (map reading Garmin), extra tools, bullhorns."

Bear gave me one of his *what about my cookies?* looks, and I reassured him that his blue box of freeze-dried liver and collapsible water dish were in the trunk, all the while thinking that I had neglected to pack a dinner for him. I always cooked Bear's evening meal, offering him steak, roast beef, or chicken.

I then reviewed my list of "forgotten" personal items. I usually kept a change of clothes with my emergency gear, but I had overlooked packing a pair of long trousers. I naively thought that another day in the same shorts I was wearing, if it came to that, wouldn't matter. It was a warm day (temperatures had been in the seventies), and I was wearing my marine safety uniform of cargo shorts and a tee shirt. I also made note that I did not have my blood pressure medication with me. It was something I occasionally forgot to take, and at the time I shrugged off my omission.

I was mid-way down the West Side Highway when the NPR announcer broke the news that the Pentagon had been hit. It was now clear: The United States of America was at war. There were only emergency vehicles on the road, and most of us were heading south, toward the World Trade Center. I think we all pressed a little harder on our accelerators after that news.

Strange, seemingly disjointed, thoughts must have invaded everyone's mind that morning. As I raced past the USS Intrepid Sea-Air-Space Museum, the refurbished WWII aircraft carrier permanently docked along the Hudson River, my heart beat a little harder. I thought about the young sailors who had perished when kamikazes exploded into the then-wooden deck half a century ago, nearly destroying it. Although many men died, and many more were injured, the Intrepid's sailors fought a heroic battle for survival. Their ship went to a near forty percent list, only to be righted and saved by teamwork, courage, and strong leadership. Now, the people of New York City were being asked to fight modern kamikazes. The similarities of that day to today overwhelmed me, and a lump rose in my throat.

As we drew closer to the World Trade Towers, I again contemplated which agency I should report to. As a volunteer, and not an active member of any organization, I wanted to maximize my use, not just add to the congestion of responders. Most recently I had worked as a marine safety consultant for the New York City Urban Parks Department. I thought that I might either report to them or to the Red Cross or FEMA. I tried calling all three on my cell phone but quickly discovered the lines were still jammed. Ultimately, I assumed that I would be used in a support function of some type, logistics being my specialty.

Ironically, what never crossed my mind and what I had never considered, was that I would be involved in rescue work, especially search and rescue work with Bear. On the morning of September 11th, I was only thinking in terms of disaster management, and how I could make myself useful to the authorities in charge. Bear was with me for the simple reason that he was always by my side.

When I arrived at the intersection of West and Chambers Streets, my worst fear was unfolding before my eyes. An outpouring of fire, construction, and rescue vehicles flooded the side streets and highways. The massive gridlock just kept mounting by the second. Not wanting to become part of the problem, I turned and parked my car on the side of the northbound lane of the West Side Highway, so as not to block the southern route to the Trade Center. Bear and I walked along the median, watching the situation develop.

Like angry bees protecting their hive, black and yellow New York Fire Department (FDNY) turnout coats swarmed toward the inferno that had become lower Manhattan. To the north, thousands of other rescuers were pouring into the city to do battle. From where we stood, it was easy to see that traffic was rapidly becoming an insurmountable problem. More manpower was needed to both organize and direct it, so I gave the "come quickly" whistle to Bear and we ran back to the car. We then headed north to the New York City Parks Police Headquarters on Pier 40 to request their assistance.

Providence works in strange ways. The first person I ran into at the pier was the Commissioner of Parks' Enforcement, Jack Linn. I explained the traffic problem, and he understood immediately. The Commissioner knew me from the water events I had worked, and asked an officer from communications who was standing nearby to accompany me back to Chambers Street. While I drove, Officer Bernie Solomon (now New York City Police Department (NYPD)) radioed ahead to recruit more Parks police. They were at our disposal in a matter of minutes.

Once back at West and Chambers Street, I secured the same space in the northbound lane as I had earlier. Strangely, over the course of the next six weeks I was always able to return to this same parking spot close to the site. A parking space may seem like a trivial bit of New York City minutia, given all that was happening, but in the days that followed I considered myself blessed whenever I needed a piece of emergency equipment from my amazingly close-at-hand car.

By the time we had returned the South Tower had collapsed. You could feel the urgency and adrenaline rising among the rescuers as they scrambled for directions and accurate information. As often happens in a crisis, many of the people who should have been in charge were overwhelmed. The hierarchy of command had temporarily broken down, and ordinary police officers and volunteers were stepping up to the plate to infuse order into the chaos. Rank had little or no meaning; it was a matter of who could get the job done. I learned better than in any class I had taken that, in a crisis, people look for leadership, not rank. In these first hours the natural leaders showed the way. Since 9/11 I've never looked at rank quite the same way again.

At this point, I took out what became one of my most valuable tools, a bullhorn. The cacophony of engines, shouts, horns, and wailing sirens made it impossible to be heard normally. (I have often thought that sirens give those in emergency services comfort in these frightening moments.) Then, with maybe two dozen Parks' police, NYPD, and even Guardian Angels, we instructed vehicles to drop off personnel and equipment and then go through the U-turn at Chambers Street to park farther north along the side of the north bound lane of the West Side Highway. In the first days of the tragedy I went through eight bullhorns. I had never realized that they could wear out, but through hours of squeezing them with all my might they did.

While I worked, Bear surveyed the scene. He stood vigilant and alert, calmly taking in the frenetic activity that encircled him. The transition from country to city never flustered Bear. He was at home in both worlds. If the exhaust fumes, dirt, dust, and ash bothered him he didn't show it. As tense as the situation was, I was amazed at the number of rescuers who streamed by, pausing to give Bear a pat on the head. "Hey fella," or "Great looking dog," they said, stopping for a moment to stroke his fur. In some cases, just the sight of Bear made the muscles in their faces relax for a brief second or two. Later, on the pile, there were many moments when Bear and the other dogs provided a kind of reassuring solace to these brave men and women.

Like so many others who were there, I have no true sense of the time when events occurred. I only know that I was directing traffic when the North Tower fell. There was no explosion. I recall I heard a low deep rumble like a freight train, or thunder echoing through the mountains. Then came a swooshing sound, like the kind white water rapids make cutting through a canyon. That must have been the steel and thousands of glass windows coming down from the tower. The mass of humanity—volunteers, rescuers, victims, and Bear and I—began running north. We all thought the tower was going to topple over on us. I screamed over the roar to Bear the command to come quickly: "Oso, rapido. Pronto!" We ran 100 or 120 yards up the highway before we stopped and turned to watch the scene behind us unfold. Gray dust rolled like a desert sand storm in our direction. *This is it,* I thought, *we're going to be hit by debris or asphyxiated.* It was like the whole world had stopped and hung for a moment in mid-air. Miraculously, we were far enough away.

I was relieved that Bear didn't get spooked. He stood, head held high, nose to the wind, as if mesmerized by what he could see, hear, and smell. Through all these days of hell, Bear never lost his dignified manner. He remained a model of self-composure.

As for me, a voice in my head kept saying, *this isn't happening, not in New York, not in America.* I could read these same thoughts on the faces of the rescuers around me. At the time only Bear was measuring, analyzing, and applying all of his canine abilities to make sense out of this new world. That was one of the incredible things about the dogs on the site: they utilized every ounce of skill, training, and ability to do their job in the moment. We all learned a lot from working with them.

As the dust settled, everyone gathered their wits and quickly went back to work. The Chief of the Emergency Services Unit (ESU) came up to me and asked to borrow my bullhorn. He's a big powerful man and the kind of leader who instills confidence in his men. I could see that easing the gridlock was also his priority so I handed my bullhorn over to him. There were plenty of police directing traffic now, and I was free to leave.

I looked uptown. The sky remained a flawless shade of blue, and the Hudson River sparkled in the sunlight. A variety of vessels were cutting through the water, headed north and west, away from Manhattan. Even the New Jersey shoreline looked peaceful. It could have been just another exquisite day in early autumn. But when I looked south, down West Street, the landscape was dramatically different. The world was blanketed in a dull gray fog. The heaviest dust and smoke was blowing south and eastward away from us toward

Brooklyn Heights by the prevailing winds.

For the first time that day I suddenly realized that Bear and I would need to call on our search and rescue training. As I thought about our abilities, I knew that in some small way we might be of help. It wasn't until I looked down at Bear that I felt a wave of raw fear come over me. I had no idea of what we would find at the disaster site, I only knew it would be a tough go.

Since Honey had died, Bear was my whole life. I heard myself blurt out loud, *Am I killing the only thing I have left that I love?* Then, along with hundreds of others, we began the grim walk in. I prayed that all the subtle lessons of a lifetime would see us through.

FINDING THE CHIEF

There were no human sounds.

This was the thought that kept turning over and over again in my head. I'd been at a party a block away from Ground Zero only three days earlier, but now I couldn't recognize a street, a building, or signpost. Bear and I could have just as easily been standing on the moon.

The whole downtown area was a lunarscape coated in gray and white ash. Only hissing fires and the occasional explosions from severed electrical and gas lines punctuated the futile wailing of sirens in the distance. Debris was still falling. Pieces the size of cars and small trucks were breaking away from the sides of buildings and crashing into smoldering pits of steel and crushed concrete.

Smoke and dust from the second tower's collapse obliterated the landscape. It was impossible to tell if parts of the building were left standing or not. Strangely, I can't recall seeing any wood: no chairs or desks or furniture of any kind. Yet there was paper everywhere: computer printouts, ledger sheets, jotted memos, personal receipts, and all the minutia of day-to-day business. Thousands of pieces fluttered in the air. I later learned they had been released on impact when the planes hit, thus escaping the implosion and incineration. Now they were left to drift to earth, adding to this bitter place.

I was disoriented. Like my co-rescuers, I was certain that once we entered this hell we would not come out of it unharmed. Then I looked at Bear, expecting him to be skittish. He was as calm and composed as if we were taking a walk in the park. A group of fire-fighters stood near to us. They gave me a puzzled look, and then their gaze fell on Bear. To see a golden retriever standing unflinchingly at the gates of hell must have seemed incongruous, if not ludicrous. Then they shook their heads as if to say, *if this dog can walk calmly forward then we're with him.* More than once during those next few days it was man's best friend who helped to give all of us the courage to go on and the knowledge of where to proceed.

When West Street became impassable, Bear and I entered the World Financial Center American Express Building, which was still standing. My goal was to work our way through the buildings to a more southerly point on West Street to gain better access to the devastated area. In those first days that I was at Ground Zero, I never knew the names of all of the buildings. A lot of us simply referred to them by the way they looked and their location—for example, "The structure at the southeast end with the ripped-open side." Members of the media walked the periphery of the site with maps. More than once I mused over the fact that everyone else in the world knew where we were except those of us helping out at the site! I myself had been working in and around the vicinity of lower Manhattan twice a week in the six months before the event, and yet I had no frame of reference for where I standing. It wasn't until later in the week, when maps were printed of the site, that I learned what the buildings there were called. It might sound peculiar, but with everything we all saw and felt at Ground Zero there is a part of me that, to this day, does not want to know the proper names of the buildings.

Bear and I made our way through the dust-choked corridors of the World Financial Center. Desks were neatly arranged with opened newspapers and half-filled coffee cups. In some cases, even briefcases and laptop computers were lying open, ready for their work-a-day tasks. We checked offices and even a bank for victims. I recall looking out of a window onto the debris field and seeing what I thought was a body lying there. Bear occasionally stopped to sniff or listen, and I called out to see if anyone might be left in the building, but it was clear that it was deserted of employees. We met other res-cuers in the hallways and we stopped to quickly compare notes about casualties and the building's structural integrity. Everything seemed to be satisfactory.

Once I was confident that no one remained, we circled back towards the entrance of the building. I had stopped to wash the dust and ash out of Bear's eyes and nostrils when a big guy approached me and asked if Bear was a search dog. It was obvious that he was a New York City Fireman. Not only did he look like the prototype of one, with his wide mustache, rugged face, and well-used turnout coat, but he had the calm and in-control demeanor all of these men and women possess, no matter what the danger. He introduced himself as "T.J. Munday from Engine Company 35" and said that he had come looking for his fallen brothers. He asked if Bear and I could help him search the debris.

You size up people quickly in my line of work, and I could see he wore his strength of character well. I figured this would be a good man to walk into hell with, so I followed him back through the Amex building. Months later, I had a chuckle when I learned that his first impression of me, wading through the ash and rubble in shorts and a "marine safety" shirt with a golden retriever, was that I was "some kind of kook." At the time, T. J. didn't know what casualties the FDNY had taken, and he wondered if he would get into trouble with the Chief for taking "a civilian and his dog" onto the disaster site.

In retrospect, I realized that the firemen were not used to working with search and rescue dogs. In fact, there were occasions in those first hours when even the fire chiefs didn't know what to do with Bear and me, and they would look at me strangely as if they were wondering, *what's a guy with a dog doing here?* I give T.J. Munday a lot of credit for having the foresight and presence of mind to recognize that a search dog would be an invaluable asset in the rubble. I have often wondered why even after the World Trade Center disaster the FDNY has not recruited search and rescue canines—or even arson dogs. Fire marshals that I have spoken with have told me that they would love to have these K-9 investigators at their disposal but, at this writing, no such investment has been made.

We made small talk as we walked. He said that he was off-duty when he heard about the attack and, knowing the streets would be impassable, had his brother transport him by boat from Brooklyn to North Cove Harbor in Battery Park. I thought to myself, *now here's a guy who knows how to improvise.*

When we got to the World Trade Center's atrium, the Winter Garden, we found it demolished. The breathtaking ten-story atrium had crumbled and the floor was filled with a mixture of steel and glittering piles of safety glass. In some places the debris was four stories high and had come bursting down the staircase, filling the West Street side. We waded through to the escalator and walked down. I think we both broke a sweat by the time we got to the south building. Eventually, we waded through to a bottom floor window that led out to West Street. Firefighters from Engine Company 14 had knocked it out as an access route in the first minutes after the second tower collapsed. (It took three days before I realized that this room we continued to enter and exit the pile from had been an exercise gym.) When we got to the window a young firefighter was standing nearby and offered his help. Although I later discovered that Jon-Paul Augier had been in the department for two years, he looked too young even for the academy. After seeing him interviewed many months later on television, my women friends were quick to inform me that he has "Hollywood good looks."

T. J. started to help me lift Bear through the window when a concerned look passed over his face. "Are you sure you want to do this to your dog?" he said. "The metal is like razor blades out there. He might get hurt." Then he asked me if Bear had boots. I replied no, but that Bear and I could both take a cut or two. T.J. then climbed through the window and motioned for me to pass Bear to him.

When we stepped out onto solid ground the debris pile rose up like a wave in front of us, obliterating the sight of West Street for as far as we could see in both directions. The rubble must have been 30 to 40 feet high in places, and there was no indication that a highway (West Street) had ever existed. I could make out what I thought was the Marriott Hotel smoldering across from us. Here and there I caught glimpses of fire rigs and ambulances that had rushed to the scene, only to be crushed under the steel and concrete. Bodies of victims were visible and quickly being attended to. There was one rig close by, turned on its side with the jump seats facing us. Rescuers, caked in dust and ash, were crawling all over it trying to reach the bodies of two firemen who had perished inside. There were also utility vehicles, mostly government-owned, scattered everywhere. Each one was being carefully searched for victims. We joined a few firemen gathered near a small depression on the pile. I'll never know what compelled us to walk in this direction…but I'll always believe it was an act of Providence.

The depression we had stopped in was covered with scattered paperwork. Some of the world's most powerful corporations were housed in the World Trade Center, and the papers that recorded so many millions in corporate assets were meaningless now and trampled on in the frantic search for human life. We stood there for only a few moments when I noticed that Bear was sniffing at one of these small pieces of paper. The way that he wouldn't leave it alone was his signal to me that he detected blood. I paused and picked it up. It was, in fact, flecked with dried blood. He began aggressively nosing the area where we had gathered, shoving his snout down into the mangled pieces of metal and concrete. Something had captured his interest. When Bear is on to a scent he is single-minded about it. His ears are forward and every muscle and sinew in his body tenses with anticipation. We all watched motionless as he began circling, and then narrowing his circle, keying in on the depression in the same area where we had gathered. He paused several times to sniff the air, but then eagerly returned to follow a scent on the ground. I knew he was going to make a hit.

"Bubba, find the baby," I said. "Go find the baby."

T.J. gave me a funny kind of look. I explained that I had trained Bear to search with this command because everybody is somebody's baby. T.J. nodded and I could see tears welling up in his eyes.

Much later that night I too would understand the difference a few words can make to the human spirit. I was searching a void with another canine team that was part of a large group I was leading. There must have been at least twenty-five or thirty FDNY looking expectantly down on us in the void when I heard a handler say to his dog, "Find the dead guy." My heart sank when I saw the devastated look that passed across the faces of the firemen.

Suddenly Bear indicated by scratching the ground with his right paw. "He's got a hit," I said.

"Are you sure?" T.J. looked skeptical. I nodded. Not only did Bear indicate with his right paw when he made a hit but he always froze in position and kept his nose wedged into the ground.

T.J. called other firemen over to help. Within minutes there were thirty or forty guys furiously digging and moving large chunks of rubble. One of my best friends, Joe Hudak, an FDNY paramedic instructor who is considered one of the best in the country, was among those unearthing the debris. They had been digging for several minutes when I realized that Bear and I could do nothing more to assist. Standing around wasn't efficient use of our time. Along with Jon-Paul Augier, we moved on to search other spots. The devastation was so extensive and there were so many casualties that I knew we needed to put a time-motion methodology into play. This wasn't about waiting around for a pat on the back for being right; it was about maximizing resources to find the most victims we could locate.

I knew that Bear would be put to best use by moving on to more "finds" rather than waiting to see the outcome of his indications, so I instructed him to continue searching. As the rescuers grew confident in Bear's accuracy and followed-up on his "alerts" I grew certain that this was our best working method.

I never learned the outcome of Bear's first find. However, nine months later, my friend, former Deputy Commissioner of Public Works and Chief of Operations of Westchester County, Arthur Freed, contacted me and told me that Dennis Smith had detailed Bear's recovery of New York City Fire Department Chief Peter Ganci (as described by T.J. Munday, in his book, *Report from Ground Zero*). Bear located too many victims in his days on the site, but I will always believe now that fate led the first search and rescue dog in the area to find the beloved Chief, the first buried hero he located.

During that first day Jon-Paul and I stayed together for only an hour. During this time Bear made three more finds of buried victims. (There were many bodies visible and already being attended to.) They were all civilians, we believe. And nose to the ground, Bear never stopped for a moment. Jon-Paul described it best in an interview he later gave for the Comcast Cable Network:

> "It was like being on the moon. Bear was working as hard as we were. The debris field was so large we didn't know where to start. It was overwhelming for all of us. Only a dog could show us where to search, and Bear was the only dog I saw working the first day. He was phenomenal. I wanted to keep him with me, but the other firemen were trying to latch on to him too. Everybody wanted Bear. I was amazed that a search dog was on the site working so soon after the second building's collapse."

Ground Zero at night under the lights set up by the
motion picture lighting crews.
(Tom Fletcher)

West Street at night
(Tom Fletcher)

Looking out at the pile from one of the still standing structures.
(Tom Fletcher)

Bear never accepted food from strangers until the
first night at Ground Zero when he ate ten steak
sandwiches from a salvation army volunteer.
(Sue Flis)

When Bear received the "Hero Dog of the Year Award" at the Annual International Cat Show in White Plains, New York, I smiled for the first since 9/11. Just the idea of the cats honoring the dogs....

Bear was honored by the Society of Illustrators. Steve Parton, an award winning artist, created a painting of Bear and me on the pile. This work traveled across the United States with the 9/11 exhibition, "The Prevailing Human Spirit."

Bear and I were honored to help the American Cancer Society's Annual "Dogswalk" Bear is enjoying a pat on the head from New York City Commissioner of Parks, Adrian Benepe.
(Tony Wladyka)

Chief Martin, Director FDNY/EMS Academy, Fort Totten, New York, Joe Hudak, EMS Instructor, Theodore, and Scott Shields, at Fort Totten. On September 11, 2004, in a ceremony at the FDNY/EMS Academy to honor the fallen heroes of 9/11, a brick was placed in the Wall of Fallen Heroes inscribed with Bear's name. (Jared Ring)

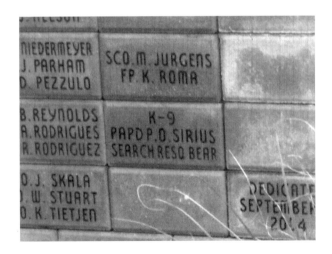

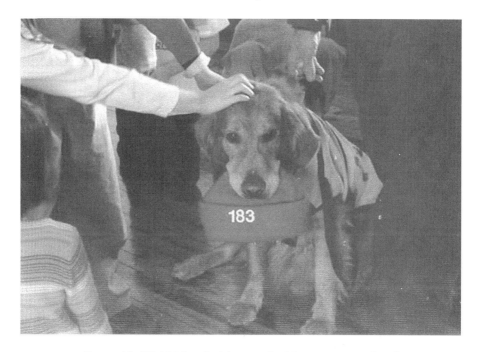

Bear with PS 183 hat in his mouth. My grammar school honored us by using this photo as the cover of their 2002 yearbook.
(Eric Byrne)

Eventually, Jon-Paul returned to the area of the Financial Center to look for T.J. Munday. After we went our separate ways, I never worked with either of them again although we waved hello when we spotted one another over the next several weeks. It wasn't until many months later that I learned that young, earnest-faced Jon-Paul Augier had been involved with one of the most heroic rescues of that day. After evacuating everyone out of his building, Joe Webber, Special Agent In Charge U.S. Customs Service, New York (adjacent to One World Trade Center, also referred to as the North Tower) found himself trapped on the seventh floor. Half of the building had been ripped away and pushed below street level when the North Tower came down. Jon-Paul and several other firefighters were near-by when Webber threw an office chair out of the window to attract attention. They looked up to see him waving desperately from a window. Knowing that the building was in jeopardy of collapsing, not to mention that it housed large amounts of confiscated and highly combustible ammunition (evidence that was supposed to be used in court cases), Jon-Paul and his partners climbed to the seventh floor to Mr. Webber's aid. When I finally met Jon-Paul again in the summer of 2002 and told him how proud I was of his heroism, the twenty-six-year-old humbly shook his head and said, "I'm not any more a hero than anyone else. We were all just firemen doing our job."

The humbleness of New York City firefighters always amazes me, but Jon-Paul and T.J. will forever be my personal heroes.

COAST GUARD TO THE RESCUE

The ash and dust was debilitating. It invaded our eyes, our noses, even our ears. As bad as it was for us (most of us didn't wear masks that first day), it was even more hazardous for the dogs. With his nose tirelessly rooting through what was often a foot of ash, I worried that Bear would inhale too many toxins, or even asphyxiate from the soot he breathed in. I stopped at least once an hour to rinse his eyes, wipe out his ears, clean his pads, and try to wash the ash from his nostrils. The first day all I had to clean his nose with was a bottle of water. When the veterinarians arrived to help out later on, they routinely suctioned out the soot that was jammed in Bear's nostrils.

It was during one of our respites at the temporary triage center that had been set up at Stuyvesant High School (armies of doctors and nurses had rushed to Ground Zero to set-up these makeshift medical units) that I noticed the cots were filled with firefighters. This struck me as odd because we weren't taking on casualties from the rubble pile. "Where did all of these guys come from?" I asked one of the doctors. "I haven't seen problems like this on the site."

"Oh, they're not from the site," she said. "They're mostly from the West Side Highway."

These men and women were experiencing cardiac complications and heatstroke from carrying hundreds of pounds of equipment down the open highway in the September heat. The gridlock we had kept at bay the first morning had inevitably grown. Rescuers were hand-carrying two and three eight-to-ten-foot-long pry bars, jaws of life, gas power saws, axes, torches, and multiple air-paks (these are comparable to scuba oxygen tanks), all while wearing full turnout gear. It was heartbreaking to see these magnificent rescuers cut down by nothing more than a logistical and transportation snag. As I looked at them an idea began to take shape in my head. Having done large event coordination of marine activities in the waters surrounding Manhattan, as well as supervising safety at dozens of large harbor events each spring and summer, I knew the boating resources that existed. It was then I realized one of the ways in which the harbor could play a significant role in the city's fate.

Bear and I left the triage center and quickly made our way along the Hudson River toward Rockefeller Park. Like a scene from a Tom Clancy novel, the once-tranquil park's greens swarmed with police and military helicopters. I was again struck with the knowledge that we were at war. The sea wall next to the park was filled with every type of water vessel, docked and waiting for what must have been evacuation orders.

I scanned the line of tugs, ferries, and police and Coast Guard boats until I saw the ship that could accomplish the mission I had in mind: to organize a shuttle service for the firefighters and other rescue workers. I spotted the CGC Katherine Walker, a state-of-the-art buoy tender, and knew she would have the communications equipment necessary to make contact with every kind of vessel in the area. I requested permission to go aboard and speak with her captain.

Several members of the crew came forward with wide grins when they saw Bear panting and caked in soot. They took him to the galley to get him water and food while I climbed up to the commanding officer on the bridge.

The captain of the ship, Steve Wittrock, along with two of his chiefs, listened to my plan. We would deploy small craft to Pier 25, the pier closest to where the gridlock started, to transport fresh rescue personnel and equipment from that point to North Cove, the marina closest to Ground Zero, and the easiest access into the site. In this way we hoped to eliminate the firefighters' exhausting march down the West Side Highway, which as the minutes wore on was growing longer and more dangerous.

Bear and I jumped off the Katherine Walker and made our way north. When we arrived at Pier 25 there was a chief of a department guarding the twenty-foot wrought iron gate. "We've got boats coming in to take rescuers and equipment to North Cove," I explained.

"No way, we've got orders to secure the piers. No one passes," was the response. Word had gone out that terrorists were planning to take over the river's access. I died a little inside, but this kind of paranoia, some well-founded, was everywhere those first few days—if not months after the tragedy.

"Listen," I said, "We've got a fleet of ships headed for this pier and we need to get through." By this time, the Parks Enforcement Police, NYPD, National Guard, and Guardian Angels had joined us. I turned toward them and shouted an order for them to remove the officer. They looked at me and hesitated for a second. It was one of the longest seconds in my life. Suddenly a Parks' Officer, a big guy named Officer Gee, stepped forward. The other officers followed, and together they picked the chief up bodily to clear the way.

I grabbed a bullhorn and began shouting, "Fire to the pier! We've got boats to take you to the site!" and diverted firemen from the highway to the water. I'll always remember the looks on the faces of these rescuers as they gathered with tense but relieved expressions to wait for a transport to the site. It was then that I had a fleeting but terrible thought: *I wondered what I would say to them if the Coast Guard never arrived.*

One of the most memorable moments of my life will always be when I turned around to see a convoy of Coast Guard ships and at least fifty other boats cutting through the Hudson River toward the pier. Chief Steve Worrell of the Katherine Walker jumped off the first boat with radio in hand to direct the landing of the boats. The operation went smoothly, and the men's grim faces broke into smiles when Bear greeted them with a welcoming wag as they boarded.

Exhausted, Bear and I hitched a ride on the last boat back to North Cove. We had just settled down for the short rest when we had one of those small- world experiences that can happen even in hell. The boat was loaded with 25 to 30 construction and rescue workers, and I noticed that two firemen sitting in the stern were staring at us. They were dressed in turnout gear too stylish to be FDNY, so I suspected they were from a well-to-do out-of-town unit.

The boat captain explained to them that I was the guy who had come up with the idea to put the shuttle system together. "Hey, Scott," one of them finally called out, "don't you recognize us? Last month we saved your ass when your house was in two feet of water. Thanks for saving ours tonight."

I must have looked puzzled because he went on, "Don't you remember? When your house flooded we got you out." Then I recognized them. It was true. Our home had been the victim of a water main break, and this Greenwich, Connecticut unit had come to our rescue. Bear and I often seemed to live serendipitous lives, and our days at Ground Zero were no exception.

SURROUNDED BY FRIENDS

It's difficult to describe what it feels like to walk onto a battlefield and find oneself surrounded by friends. These were friends who only hours earlier were ordinary men and women going about their daily business, and then suddenly discovered that they were willing to risk everything in the service of others. There were countless volunteers in the harbor during those days, and Bear and I had been privileged to call many of them our friends even before the events of 9/11. One such friend, and perhaps one of the biggest heroes of that and the ensuing days, was the fireboat (and crew), the John J. Harvey. The Harvey, a one-hundred-thirty-foot fireboat originally built in 1931, was retired in 1995 and sold by the city for $50,000 as scrap in 1999. A team of dedicated volunteers worked on the tug to make this old lady seaworthy.

Today, the Harvey is not only seaworthy, but she's become a legend. A month before the World Trade Center disaster the Harvey was used as the committee boat for the annual tug boat races held in New York Harbor. All the new and current tugs were lined up on the Harvey. As a safety officer for the event, I was standing on the bridge with Captain Huntly Gill waiting for the competition to begin when he got this impish grin on his face: "Let's race," he said. He threw the telegraph down to Tim Ivory, the engineer, and he fired up the engines. Tim, who had dedicated the last few years of his life to rebuilding the Harvey (even though he was often asked to work on other boats for more money), must have read Huntly's mind and pushed the engines to their max. To everyone's amazement, the old lady who was there to host the event came in first against all the new tugs. Little did any one realize that her best days were still to come....

Minutes after planes flew into the Trade Towers the crew of the Harvey spontaneously met at Pier 63 where she lies anchored. Her first mission was to rescue 150 ash-covered souls, many of them dressed in business suits and in a state of shock. They were trapped near the sea wall on the Battery, and the Harvey ferried them to safety. The crew had barely completed their mission when an FDNY dispatcher requested they return to North Cove where they ran water lines between the World Financial Center buildings to the site.

This was necessary because soon after the Trade Towers were hit there was no water left in downtown Manhattan. The sprinkler systems in the buildings had depleted the ready supply, and there were cracked water mains and water line ruptures everywhere. There was no water to fight the fires surrounding us. The Harvey is capable of pumping 18,000 gallons of water per minute, and along with the Firefighter and the McKean, New York's two other fireboats, she pumped water from the Hudson River for the next 80 hours. Today, if you visit New York you can tour the Harvey at Pier 63. It's a terrific stop for the whole family. Both kids and adults love to take rides on the old fireboat and watch her water cannons shoot 150-foot sprays.

Another friend of Bear's and mine was the Chelsea Screamer, a fifty-mile-an-hour tour boat owned by Sean and Tommy Kennedy. From the first hour of the tragedy, the Screamer ferried people to safety from lower Manhattan. With area bridges and tunnels shut down (not to mention the gridlock), they transported emergency rescue workers back to North Cove. The Screamer uses a tremendous amount of gas, but the owners never thought about the money and paid for fuel out of their own pockets. They volunteered their boat for service for as long as it was needed. I felt fortunate that Bear and I were often their passengers during the rescue efforts.

The Kennedy brothers also own a yacht called the Mariner III, probably one of the most beautiful charter motor yachts in New York

Harbor, and they generously welcomed rescuers to stay aboard. They hosted a US Army rescue team the first night, and offered the same to anyone who wanted a place to catch a rest in the ensuing weeks. There were several nights when Bear and I were fortunate enough to spend the night aboard the Mariner. Bear was content to bed down anywhere, but I must admit I could easily be spoiled staying in one of her sumptuous staterooms, and eating the incredible gourmet meals cooked by Tommy Kennedy.

The Spirit Line Cruises were huge tour boats used for dinner cruises. They were tied to the west side of North Cove, and initially were set up as triage centers. They then became respite sites where rescue workers could freshen up either before or after working on the site. Some of the country's best chefs were recruited to provide meals aboard these ships. Director of Marine Operations Greg Hanchrow coordinated these activities. As with the Mariner III, I know it took the Spirit Line months to repair the damage and wear and tear created by the heavy rescue gear and apparatus dragged on and off the luxury vessel in the weeks following the World Trade Center disaster.

North Cove, along with Pier 40 on the West Side Highway, became the center point for logistics. Captain Greg Freitas of the Adirondack, an eighty- foot majestic-looking sloop and the most beautiful charter sailboat in the harbor, set up one of the largest logistical dumps on the south side of North Cove. This site was so well run that a site operated by the government was eventually eliminated at everyone's request, and Greg stayed on to do logistics. In the days before the World Trade Center tragedy Greg loved to take Honey and Bear out for cruises on the Adirondack to entertain his clientele.

The Horizon Cruise Ship line also evacuated thousands of stranded New Yorkers to safety from lower Manhattan. John Krevey, who owns Pier 63, a four-hundred-foot entertainment complex, supplied the Harvey and others with provisions. Patrick Harris, captain of the Ventura, another fabulous sloop, also devoted his services for many weeks. The list of heroes goes on.

Not enough can be said for the importance of New York's waterways and the volunteer boats and crews who worked them in the days and weeks after the tragedy. The men and women of the rivers and harbors applied their mariners' expertise in dealing with the disaster. They understood the importance of coordination and cooperation. Their efforts flew in the face of the chaos that permeated the first hours of the tragedy, and their continued organized manpower and resources provided invaluable services to the city, its citizens, and its work force in the long weeks after the tragic event.

It's without question that should the island of Manhattan ever again come under attack, the waterways would once again play a critical role, and these "volunteer and professional responders" from the private sector would be some of the very first to answer the call for help. To this end, it's important for diverse agencies to begin working together now to construct a "what if" plan for the future, a "what if plan" that, hopefully, will never have to be implemented. As my friend, Robert Pouch, Director, Board of Commissioners of Pilots for the State of New York, explained in a talk on traffic and communications in New York Harbor at a marine rescue training session hosted by the USS Intrepid and the New York City Urban Parks Search and Rescue Team, "It's important for both the private sector and the local and federal government to work together to coordinate their resources in the event of a catastrophic emergency. When we look at homeland security this kind of inter-agency training and preparedness can make a critical difference."

NEW YORK CITY PARKS POLICE AND RANGERS

Bear and I were fortunate to know and work with many of the folks in the Parks Department as a result of my safety work at harbor events. These individuals also played a vital role in the rescue and recovery efforts from the first moments of the tragedy until many months afterwards. From Director Sara Hobel of the Parks Rangers to Chief Alex Brash of the Parks Police, they assembled their officers and rapidly responded to the call for help.

Several dozen Parks Enforcement Police had gathered in Battery Park on the morning of September 11th to participate in a department-wide training program. As Commissioner Jack Linn of Parks Enforcement describes:

"Several dozen Parks employees were enjoying the exceptionally beautiful day and chatting over their morning coffee before the training started when a jumbo jet soared into the North Tower a block away. Everyone was stunned. Then the second plane hit the South Tower. One of my officers had family members working in both buildings. It was awful. But because of the fact that we had our regular Battery Park Police on duty along with many more on site for the training, we moved into full operation immediately. By eleven o'clock we had 80 to 90 officers working at Ground Zero. Because we have security contracts with both the residential sector as well as the World Financial

Center our role was well-defined from the outset. We secured the waterfront bulkhead for both the evacuation and supply efforts, and the fireboat access. We also set up helicopter landing pads for the police and military. We were also able to provide transportation for supplies and equipment, organize volunteer efforts, and help re-establish command posts and communication bases for the NYC Office of Emergency Management that had been located in Building Seven of the World Trade Center complex and destroyed in the building's collapse.

Some of our most rewarding work, however, was rescue. We rescued over one thousand pets from abandoned apartments in those first few days: dogs, cats, guinea pigs, rabbits, hamsters, birds, fish, and lizards. It was incredible, but other than one dead goldfish and a cat that was killed when a piece from one of the planes crashed through the window of the apartment where it was living, we only lost one pet, a dog. We were transporting a small dog to safety on the back of a truck when we hit a bump in the road and its crate popped open. I happened to be on the truck at the time. Two officers tried to catch the dog but it bit both of them and got away. I chased it up and down several blocks. I even had several firefighters join in the chase. But he was too fast for all of us. We chased him all the way to the Ground Zero pit, where he disappeared into the rubble.

Another equally rewarding part of our work was escorting the thousands of residents back to their apartment buildings to gather whatever personal possessions (such as clothing and medications) they could carry out with them. These folks would wait for hours and then have to hike over debris and fire hoses to get to their buildings. These buildings were without electricity, which meant they sometimes had to climb twenty to forty floors up blackened stairwells to get to their apartments. We had so many residents to escort that we had to limit their time in their homes to just fifteen minutes each. It was amazing, though, because they were so thrilled and appreciative to have those few short minutes. The difference between how they looked and acted before and after they visited their homes was astounding."

Today, in part as a result of their work during the disaster, the Parks Department has a search and rescue team staffed with a dozen professional members as well as twenty-five highly qualified volunteers and half a dozen canines. This team works in coordination with other agencies throughout New York City. It provides Ground and Mobile SAR teams, Technical Rope Rescue, Marine Rescue, Animal Rescue, K-9 SAR and bomb K-9's, and Special Events coverage.

The first year anniversary September 11, 2002.
Bear and I are standing with three search and rescue
canine teams. (left to right: Dale Warke and sasha, Frederick Golba and
Ammo. Me with Bear, and Joe Paulfrey with Roscoe.)
(Richard Cohen)

THE HEROES' HIGHWAY

They arrived by the thousands that first afternoon, and many of them stayed on until the last rescue workers departed more than a year later. The citizen volunteers of the West Side Highway were like a cheerleading squad boosting the moral of the army of rescue workers that passed along its route, traveling to and from Ground Zero. In the early days of the tragedy these folks provided food, water, towels, blankets, tarps, deodorant, soap, eyewash, razor blades, gloves, helmets, flashlights, hand tools, and just about anything else that could make life go a little bit smoother. In fact, these citizen logistics sites were so efficient and lent themselves to expediency rather than red tape (there's nothing worse than filling out government forms to requisition a tube of toothpaste when you're on a search and rescue mission!) that most of the emergency rescue workers I met chose to utilize the civilian-run depots. When supplies were no longer needed, many remained to continue a goodwill vigil. They stood in the median of the highway and applauded rescuers with smiles, waves, and "Thank you!" signs as they drove to and from their heartbreaking work.

On the second night at about three in the morning, I pulled over to this cheering crowd. An elegantly-dressed gray-haired woman approached my car. She came up to my driver's window holding a large sterling silver tray of food. "Would you like some dinner?" she asked with a genteel smile. I looked down at my filthy clothing and hands. She must have read my thoughts because she then said she would be quite honored if I accepted her offer. That night I ate a delicious home-cooked meal on the side of the highway, which she served to Bear and me on fine bone china. I couldn't help but think that they should rename this highway "Heroes' Highway" for all of the men and women who worked or rode its corridors. The people of New York City banded together and did things the right way from the goodness of their hearts. I was never prouder to be an American.

ON THE PILE

Bear and I worked much of our time under the frequently photographed building facade that came to signify both the tragedy and the rescue efforts; it was a façade that several networks referred to as "the gates of the inferno." I'll never forget the image of that skeletal structure looming over us in the smoke and dust. From the first moments we began working we were certain this facade would collapse, killing all of us. After a few days those fingers of the façade rising slanted to the sky began to represent the whole incident to all of us. We were certain the city would leave this as a monument to what had happened there. It had a kind of ethereal quality to it—like a sacred spiritual place. It was our cathedral while we worked beneath it and around it, and it came to represent "Ground Zero" to the rest of the world. The day the city tore it down many of us wept bitterly for all it had come to represent.

Below the facade, under tons of steel, we could see the crushed remains of fire rigs, police cars, ambulances, and government vehicles of all types. We had all come to the site on foot with the little equipment we were able to carry, and everyone was desperate for more. Men were going through cutting blades like they were matches. Shouts were repeatedly heard for more gas torches. I saw seasoned firemen cry because they were so frustrated that they didn't have adequate supplies. After checking carefully for survivors, we cannibalized the wrecked vehicles that we could reach to re-equip ourselves. Like operating in a deadly game of pick-up sticks, we carefully removed pieces of twisted steel and concrete so as not to cause an avalanche of debris. Once the debris was removed men, and eventually dogs, could perform closer investigations.

The ironworkers, welders, steamfitters, and all the other trades-men who had come voluntarily to serve were god-sent angels those first few days. So were the motion picture lighting crews, who foresaw the need we would have as darkness fell. They showed up to illumi-nate the pile so we could work through the night. Like the firefight-ers and emergency rescue workers, these volunteer men and women would do anything, and routinely risked their own safety to get the job done. These were more of the unknown "heroes" of the World Trade Center. Many of us had taken the same training courses in inci-dent command, yet almost everyone, professional and layperson alike, worked together as brothers and sisters. It was as if we had trained together for years.

There's the old saying that you "fight the way you train." The need for standardized and cooperative inter-agency training is never more apparent than in a crisis, and some of the standardized national training was very apparent in this rescue operation. Most "profes-sional rescuers" talked the same language, thanks to the National Fire Academies having adapted the incident command system (ICS) and the nationalized standards for training that now exist. The ICS provides a model for command, control, and coordination of a response, and allows for a means to coordinate the efforts of indi-vidual agencies that respond to the situation. This ICS model is not only applicable to disaster sites but also to planned events such as celebrations, rock concerts, and official visits from dignitaries, to name a few. The Occupational Safety and Health Administration (OSHA) also requires that any agency, including private businesses, showing up at a HazMat (hazardous materials) site be trained in ICS. This brought a wide and necessary change in command and control to the system that was now being tested in a major and cat-aclysmic event.

Among the thousands of volunteers from all walks of life that feverishly labored on the pile, Bear and I kept meeting people we knew. It was during our first day of work on the pile when I was surprised to hear one of the welders refer to Bear by name. I was using Spanish, Bear's command language, and so I had been calling him "Oso." A welder was cutting steel near us for well over an hour, and he kept yelling out to the firemen, "Make sure Bear has water." I wondered how this masked and ash-encrusted man knew Bear's name, but we were all so focused on the work that I never stopped to ask his identity. Finally, he removed his helmet and inquired, "Scott, is Bear okay? Does he need anything?" I was astounded to discover that I had been working alongside a good friend and volunteer from the fireboat John J. Harvey, the welder, sculptor, and poet Andrew Furber (now a Senior Consultant with Booze Allen Hamilton's Satellite and Hybrid Communications team).

Andrew was one of the key volunteers who had helped to rebuild the Harvey. As soon as he heard that planes had flown into the towers he and the rest of the fireboat's crew spontaneously reported to their vessel on Pier 63. After tying up at North Cove and laying fire hoses a half-mile into the site he found that his assistance was no longer required on the Harvey, so he answered the call for welders at Ground Zero. Andrew later remembered working with us:

"I met Scott while volunteering with the retired fireboat John J. Harvey at Pier 63 in New York City. Scott plays the role of marine safety coordinator on the pier, and made significant contributions to ensuring safety there. He's the kind of fellow you want to have around in case of emergency. He's amazingly prepared, able to anticipate problems and risks, and has a gentle, respectful personality that helps people in trouble. At one point I needed a tool to repair some of the cutting equipment. I knew Scott carried a lot of tools in his ever-prepared state, and sure enough he was able to lend me exactly what I needed. The challenge was finding him again to return it to him since there were so many rescue workers there. When I started asking for Scott and describing him as the fellow with the rescue dog, I was able to find him fairly easily.

Scott, Bear, and I interacted frequently during the course of the week. We were friends before meeting on the pile, and we were excited to see people we recognized from different times. Scott and Bear were clearly working very hard, putting in extraordinary hours and focused on saving lives. At some point in the chaos the three of us were taking a break on the waterfront. I couldn't imagine how poorly Bear must have been doing since all of us had dust masks, but he had his nose down in the thick of it the whole week.

Bear shares the same characteristics as Scott. Just observing him on the pile and comparing him to some of the other rescue dogs, he was clearly in his element. He was at peace, agile, and didn't slow down until it was time to rest. Other dogs, I noticed, behaved erratically, emotionally, and were so apparently overwhelmed with the amount of possible bodies that they were less effective. Watching Bear and Scott interact told me something about their relationship and personalities. They were a tremendous asset to the rescue effort."

• • •

We all had some pretty rough moments on the pile, but there was one in particular that continues to haunt me to this day. At some point on the first afternoon Bear and I sat down in a small gully to take a break. While I rested Bear continued to root around in the debris. I saw him paw at something and at first I ignored it, figuring it was nothing. He kept sniffing and pawing at it so finally I went over to investigate. It looked like a thick cigar but it was pale in color. I picked it up and it unfurled in my hand. It was a scalp with soft golden blonde hair. I could tell it was a woman's because of the stylish cut. It fell out of my hand. But instead of picking it up and putting it into a HazMat bag I quickly walked away. I had seen more horrible things that day but this one really got to me. Finding something so frail and beautiful in that harsh landscape was too much of a shock for me at that moment in time. I've deeply regretted my moment of human weakness since. It had never happened to me before, and I was extremely careful to account for everything after that moment.

As for Bear, I'll never know exactly what he was thinking during these hours and days. I can easily be accused of anthropomorphizing my dog, but I believe his eyes said it all. They were pools of sadness. In fact, from September 11th until the day he died, I do not believe I ever saw a man, woman, or canine with sadder eyes. As one newscaster said on one of the national television news shows that featured Bear, "Look at those eyes! He must know something we don't know."

Bear and I posing at the North Cove memorial. This
memorial was set up by citizens and contained priceless
memorabilia from 9/11. It has now been removed.
(NYC Pet Project. Photo: Ron Monk)

SEARCH AND RESCUE (SAR) DOGS

Some of them came from as far away as western Canada, Europe, and South America. There were live find dogs and cadaver dogs, police and sheriff's dogs, and federal government dogs that joined us on the pile. In addition, volunteer search and rescue dog teams used their personal resources and dollars to travel to New York.

The dogs came in all shapes and sizes. Long noses and short snouts, prick ears and floppy ears, short legs and long fur, long legs and short fur. But they all had one thing in common: an olfactory sense thousands of times greater than a human's.

A dog's nose has two hundred million nasal olfactory receptors. Each receptor detects and identifies odor molecules that emanate from various objects. This ability to decipher and decode a kind of language that eludes us as humans makes a dog an asset of inestimable proportions on a search and rescue mission. Many of the canines at Ground Zero also had the ability to climb or to crawl into voids and crevices, some too small for the average- size man. By the end of the first day it was no secret, as Bear eloquently showed us, that the canines led the men. They were faster and more reliable than the most sophisticated search equipment.

By evening on the first night Bear was still the only dog anywhere to be seen working our section of the pile. I knew the rescuers were relying on him, but I also knew that he and I couldn't last much longer. His gait had slowed, as had mine, and every time I paused he collapsed at my feet. Ash, concrete powder, and pieces of debris blew into our faces both from the ground and from the surrounding structures. I wore a helmet most of the time, but I was worried that Bear would get hit. I kept a lookout for other dogs that would serve as reinforcements, but none appeared.

By now we were both weaving from exhaustion. One eleven-year-old dog and his middle-aged handler couldn't search so many acres and millions of pounds of rubble alone. I informed Chief Dan Nigro, who was leading the firefighters in the area where we were working, that I was going out to get more dogs and bring them back. I went out to the police command post at Stuyvesant High School, where I was told dog teams were being held in the auditorium staging area. By 'held' I mean they were not being allowed to go to Ground Zero to work. (I later heard that SAR canine teams were being held in staging areas at New York's Jacob Javits Center and in New Jersey too.)

When I reached the auditorium I was directed to an Emergency Services Unit (ESU) sergeant in charge of canine deployment. I said, "There are a thousand firefighters on the other side of that wall of rubble. They're out of communications and they need more dogs."

He looked at me like I was out of line and said, "Where's your paperwork requesting the dogs?"

"Paperwork?" I was incredulous. "Are you out of your f——-mind?" I started shouting, "This *is* Pearl Harbor—it's the start of a war! The firemen need dogs! You want *paperwork?*"

He looked at me and said, "Yeah, I need the paperwork." He shoved it at me and I had no choice but to proceed to fill it in. Then I had to take it around and get the necessary chain-of-command signatures. I never cursed in general until that night, but after that experience I think I kept on cursing for the next year. It was a heartbreaking situation, because I knew that undoubtedly the dogs would have helped the firemen tremendously in their effort to find victims sooner. When the paperwork was done I took it back to the same sergeant.

He says, "Okay, you did the paperwork but you still can't have the dogs."

At this point I was thinking, *I'm stuck in some bizarre Kafkaesque novel.* So I gave him my "the thousand firefighters over the wall of rubble and Pearl Harbor" speech all over again.

"Sorry, you need four ESU with each dog, and they've gotta be ESU. It's procedure."

I looked around and saw hundreds of cops sitting or milling around the auditorium hoping to be deployed. But they weren't ESU. I objected, "You can't put procedure ahead of people's lives! You must have three hundred police in here. Give me eight for each dog."

"I can't," he said, looking away, "They've gotta be ESU. It's procedure."

Just as I was walking out in total frustration another ESU sergeant stepped out from behind a pillar and motioned for me to step back out of sight with him. He must have overheard my exchange with the other officer, because he said, "I know who you are from the harbor. We just got in a team from Massachusetts and they haven't been checked in yet. I'll give them to you. You take them into the site and do the right thing." Although I never learned this ESU sergeant's name, he knew when to put the "rule book" aside, and he'll always be a hero to me.

I have often wondered what would have occurred had there been more search dogs on the site in those first critical hours after the disaster: Would more lives have been saved? Sadly, the closest Federal Emergency Management (FEMA) dog teams were not able to reach the site until the evening of the first day, eight to ten hours after the second building collapsed. Although these are highly trained teams, timing is everything in a crisis such as this one, and the FEMA SAR unit situated closest to New York had to travel to a Massachusetts training depot to collect equipment before traveling back to Manhattan, thus wasting precious hours that could have been used doing search and rescue work. There were also volunteer teams held in staging areas that were not allowed out on the site.

A similar situation, unfortunately, had developed after the Oklahoma City bombing. Rescue personnel on the site did not recognize the capabilities and usefulness of the canine search and rescue teams for some time. They did not understand the quantity and quality of work these dog teams could accomplish, and at first held them back from entering the site. While it's understandable that there should be control over those given access to a disaster zone, the work of these search and rescue canine teams is critical and could make the difference between life and death—especially in the first hours after a tragedy. Their role needs to be recognized by rescue agencies at all levels now, to maximize any necessary recovery efforts in future disasters.

The men and dogs I led in were from the Hamden County sheriff's department, including Michael Goldberg and his dog Jactive, and the Southbridge police department in Massachusetts. Frederick Golba and his dog Ammo, a solo volunteer team from Massachusetts, also joined us. I led these teams back over the three-story pile of rubble that I had worked on earlier that day, and we searched into the night. Bear had rested for about an hour while I went through the red tape to get more search dogs and now he was ready to go back to work. At one point Michael Goldberg looked at me a bit strangely and asked what had happened to the rest of my pants. I'd been so busy I hadn't realized that my shorts, the same shorts I had driven down from Connecticut in that morning, had been torn to shreds and my exposed legs were bruised and cut up. I explained that I had left home without a change of clothes. He led me out to his car and gave me a pair of camouflage battle dress uniform pants (BDU's). They "saved my skin," and I've kept them until this day.

It was a long night as Sergeant Brodeur of Southbridge later recalled in a telephone interview for a documentary film being done about Bear:

"We (six rescuers) arrived sometime in the afternoon but we weren't allowed to go out to the site until Captain Shields took us in that evening. The FDNY were thrilled to see us come over the pile with the dogs. I could see right away they were relying on them (the dogs). Bear was so exhausted he would make a hit and then collapse into puddles of filthy water. We lifted him into voids that still had steam pouring out of them. It was unreal. Bear was an older dog, and it broke my heart to see him work so hard, but he kept going. Sometime during the night Scott and Bear left to get some rest."

During this time Bear never wore booties. As I've mentioned, we had never trained with them, and like going to a dance in a new pair of shoes, Bear would have found them awkward and uncomfortable. I also worried that the boots might reduce his ability to maneuver safely, so I declined to use them. Luckily his pads, toughened by working the stony beaches of Long Island Sound and the hot asphalt and steel of New York's piers, held up well. The bigger problem was the pulverized concrete powder and glass that wedged between his pads and irritated them until they were inflamed. In the ensuing days I took Bear to the mobile vet unit run by the Suffolk County SPCA. They cleaned him up but then wanted to have him rest in a cage. Bear had never been in a cage in his life, and I wasn't about to let an act of terrorism put him in one, so after that I took him to the piers to hose him down and to rest along with me.

Although the human rescuers had some protection, very few of the dogs wore protective clothing. Given the sharp pieces of metal on the ground and the unstable footing, as well as debris flying off of buildings, it's nothing short of miraculous that more canines were not injured. Eventually, the site was water and mud everywhere, and the dogs were nose deep in what we all referred to as "toxic soup." Yet aside from Sirius, the bomb dog who was killed while working inside the World Trade Center, and Servus, a SAR dog who nearly suffocated on debris after falling into a pit, Mike Goldberg's Jactive, a Belgium Malinois, was one of the few severe canine casualties at the disaster site.

On the second day Mike and Jactive answered a call in the Deutsche Bank building. Word had filtered down that victims might be trapped there. A staircase collapsed, and Mike watched, horrified, as Jactive plunged through three stories. Somehow Jactive survived the fall, and was hoisted to safety. After being treated for his injuries he was taken back to Massachusetts with an NYPD motorcade where he received further treatment and recovered. He is probably the only canine to have ever received an interstate police escort.

Bear himself was injured in the rescue process. We were going up a beam when a piece of twisted metal gouged Bear's back. He always had a high tolerance for pain, so although the gash was deep, Bear kept working. I always keep a mini bottle of hydrogen peroxide with me, and I cleaned the wound from time to time. When I thought we both needed a break, I took Bear to one of the triage centers to have it cleaned and examined.

Several months later Bear developed a form of skin cancer around the perimeter of the wound. Dr Jennifer Chaitman, Director of the Veterinary Internal Medicine and Allergy Specialists of New York, successfully removed the cancerous tissue and Bear recovered. Dr. Chaitman was one of the many vets who donated services at the site. I met her at Pier 40 at the Humane Society's headquarters. She was wonderful with Bear and promised me she would take care of him for the rest of his life. Dr. Chaitman kept her promise.

On the second night, Bear was resting on a beam over a void and I was across from him sitting with my friend, Adam Brown. Adam is the CEO for Working Water Fronts, an advocacy group for public usage of New York's waterways and waterfront, and an expert rescue diver and welder. We were watching with one of the fire chiefs while rescuers checked the hole underneath with cameras and listening equipment. The men couldn't detect anything so the chief said to send Bear down. A federal canine team protested and said, "Get that mutt (Bear) out of here. Our dog here is worth fifty thousand dollars and he's one of the best in the world." I knew, and the other rescuers standing around us knew, that Bear's ability was infallible. The rescuers had seen him working and knew he always got it right. But I could see a confrontation coming, so I put my palms up and said to let their dog go in first.

We waited while their canine went down into the rubble and searched. After about ten minutes when he didn't alert they took him out. The chief again instructed me to send Bear in. The government team was insulted and repeated the monetary worth of their dog and how he was the best in the world. I saw the chief's eyes flicker with rage and he ordered them out of the void. This was no place for egos, only cooperation and team work. We had been using three and four dogs by then to check each other's work to maximize our accuracy, and to make certain we didn't get a false negative. Realizing their error, the government team skulked away. Bear went in and alerted, and another victim was recovered.

The reason this situation occurred was that certain search and rescue teams were considered 'privileged' because of their level of credentials rather than the way in which they performed on the job. Yet some of the best canines around belonged to local police and sheriffs' departments from different parts of the country. These departments may not have received national credentials, yet their teams were as rigorously trained, and performed their jobs magnificently.

In the end, a team is only as good as its dog. Credentials can be a good guidepost but it's performance that really counts. All of the canine search and rescue teams at Ground Zero took enormous risks maneuvering in the precarious and hazardous debris. Each and every team went to the site knowing they might be called upon to make the ultimate personal sacrifice, and most of these dogs accomplished their sad mission in exemplary fashion.

As the days passed and no survivors were found, many of the dogs, especially the live-find dogs, grew "depressed." The media published stories of handlers staging live rescues to boost the dogs' spirits. A note of levity was added when a sheriff from Detroit showed up at the site with a female shepherd mix in heat. Generally it's assumed that nothing is less desirable or more disruptive on a search and rescue mission than to have the male dogs distracted and trying to chase a hot female. However, there are times when the rulebook or even common sense doesn't apply to a situation. I remember thinking, *this guy is crazy bringing a dog in heat onto the site.* A lot of rescuers were even making rude comments and telling him to go home. But never did so many studs get over their depression so quickly as when that shepherd mix strolled out onto the pile. It just goes to show that you can't always tell what will work operationally, and what's thought to be a detriment can easily turn into an asset.

THE VETS

I felt fortunate to possess an assortment of skills, contacts, and knowledge that I was able to contribute to the rescue and recovery efforts in different capacities, not to mention sheer luck at being in the right place at the right time. Whether it was running into New York firefighter T.J. Munday outside the World Financial Center in that first hour after the second tower collapsed, or finding the CGC Katherine Walker to organize the ferrying of rescuers around the gridlock, I crossed paths with many heroic people that I am honored to have assisted in some small way. Dr. Barbara Kalvig, DVM and Medical Director of the New York Veterinary Hospital, was one such person.

I met Dr. Kalvig by chance at the triage center set up at the Borough of Manhattan Community College on the first afternoon. I had taken Bear there to have his eyes and nostrils cleansed, and to give him a much-needed water break. Dr. Kalvig and her team had gone to Ground Zero to assist at the human triage center. She hadn't even been thinking in terms of canine needs when she and her staff answered the call for medical help. When Dr. Kalvig saw me with Bear, she walked up to me and asked me if there was anything she could do to help the *human* victims. I could see right away that she was a vet, so I told her that I thought her efforts would be better spent taking care of the canines that I felt certain would eventually be arriving at the site. She immediately asked me what the search dogs might need. I explained some of the possible injuries I anticipated: lacerations to pads from the sharp steel, dust inhalation, dehydration, injuries from falls, and exhaustion. Dr. Kalvig said she needed to find a way to get the necessary supplies. I spotted several Drug

Enforcement Agency officers standing around looking for a mission (national disasters are not their everyday assignment!), so I asked them to escort the vets and their staffs back to Dr. Kalvig's veterinary hospital to retrieve drugs and more supplies. Additionally, the human triage center also donated supplies for canine injuries.

The vets then, along with their own staffs, packed the items into backpacks and cardboard boxes and created a mobile veterinary MASH unit. The Suffolk County SPCA Mobile Unit replaced this makeshift center the following day, and Dr. Kalvig was made chief of all veterinary and SPCA services at Ground Zero. I'm always proud to say the SPCA had the only *real* MASH unit for SAR dogs, and Bear and I were taken good care of by them in those first few days.

Over the days and weeks that followed, veterinary doctors, nurses, and staff volunteered their services around-the-clock to keep the hundreds of dogs healthy. Several animals that were rescued from the surrounding buildings were also brought to the unit. A protocol of treatment was established for all dogs. They were hydrated, something that was extremely important in those first hot weeks, and bathed immediately. Not only were the dogs working leg-deep in possible asbestos-contaminated areas, but they were also nosing into debris that contained serious pathogens. So their eyes were flushed and their ears and nostrils checked for debris. Their hearts and respiratory status were also monitored. Then their paws were closely examined for cuts, abrasions, and any imbedded shards of metal or glass.

The dogs waded through ponds of water pumped from the river by the fireboats. Although it cooled their bodies as they worked in the unsheltered heat, I worried that the bacteria from human tissue and waste that had seeped into the water would bring disease to the dogs. Over the weeks many of the dogs that continued to work the site developed diarrhea as a result of drinking contaminated water, and were treated with medication.

Over 250 veterinary volunteers and their assistants worked in the mobile hospital in the weeks that followed. Many of these volunteers would work their regular jobs and then work another twelve-hour shift at the site. Although we had federal Veterinary Medical Assistance Teams (VMAT) at Ground Zero, the scope of the disaster created needs that could not have been met without those volunteer veterinarians who aided the dogs working the disaster. The dogs never could have gotten their jobs done without them, and without the dogs the recovery of victims would have been even more painfully slow for everyone, especially those families who desperately waited for resolution.

I will always cherish this photograph. These are the
FDNY men that I walked into hell with.
Jon-Paul Augier is on the left and T.J. Munday on the right.
This was taken in July of 2002. It was the first time
I had spoken to them since September 11, 2001
(David Mintzer)

DNA *AND* SAR DOGS: *A PARTNERSHIP*

In late September of 2001, Howard Cash, President and Founder of Gene Codes Corporation, traveled from his offices in Ann Arbor, Michigan to New York City to donate existing DNA matching computer software to aid in the Chief Medical Examiner's Office identification effort. Instead, the Director of the Department of Forensic Biology, Robert Sheller, explained that the current software was not sufficient to handle the inventory of data they were collecting and they needed new technology right away. He asked if Howard would take on this seemingly impossible task. Howard returned to Michigan and presented the situation to his employees. They increased their staff, doubled their office space, and began working 24/7 to develop pattern-matching software for DNA analysis and data handling, in order to more rapidly identify the remains of those who had perished on 9/11. The software, called Mass Fatality Identification System (M-FISys), is one of several key genetic analysis tools now used by 9/11 forensic investigators, as well as labs all over the world. It keeps track of 20,000 individual remains with 14,000 samples (i.e. data derived from personal artifacts such as combs and toothbrushes) provided by grieving relatives. To date, this software has been enormously successful and has proven one hundred percent accurate.

Howard and I have become friends, and we have spoken at great length about the strange partnership that exists between the scientists and "man's best friend," and the roles that each played at Ground Zero. Without the SAR dogs, Gene Codes Forensics would never have identified as many victims as quickly as they did, and without Howard the work of the dogs would never have produced the rapid resolution that so many grieving families prayed for.

Bear and I are seated here with Lt. Steve Wittrock,
Captain of the CGC Katherine Walker
on the USS Intrepid. (New York Harbor Watch)

BLOOD PRESSURE RISING

Sometime before dawn on the second morning I went to a triage center to have my eyes and Bear's eyes washed out. We had some of the very best doctors and nurses in the world working at Ground Zero, and like all conscientious medical folks, they routinely took my vital signs. The nurse who took my blood pressure looked startled when she noted my reading, and called for a doctor's assistance. My numbers were headed off the charts, higher than they had ever been in my life. The blood pressure medication that I had neglected to pack and thought that I could live without was now required.

"I'm ordering you not to go back to the site," was the doctor's brief response when he saw my results. Then he turned to the nurse. "I'm sending him up to St. Vincent's for treatment and observation." With those words I saw ten years of emergency training going to waste.

"But I feel fine," I protested. (Except for my ankles that I had sprained and were wrapped in air casts by my friend, Tom Fletcher, an EMT from Maine, I believed I was fine.)

"You've got to go at the hospital," he responded and ended the conversation.

As the young firefighter Jon-Paul Augier later commented to me during an interview, "For an old guy you were really pushing the envelope." Young and old alike, it's what we all did during those days.

I was taken by ambulance to St. Vincent's Hospital. The floors in the emergency room were overflowing with patients sitting on makeshift chairs and lying around on the floor. I thought to myself, *so this is what a modern day emergency room looks like after an act of war.* I was turned over to Dr. Lee, who treated me. (Coincidentally, a year and a half later it was Dr. Lee who saved my sister's life when she diagnosed a medical condition that a dozen other physicians had failed to uncover.) After giving me new blood pressure medication, Bear and I were placed in the "positive pressure room." That night, Bear became the first canine to ever be treated as a patient at St. Vincent's—and they couldn't have treated us better.

The next morning, New York's Governor Pataki appeared in the entry to the positive pressure room. He was making the rounds, visiting victims and injured rescuers. As much as I have come to like the Governor, I think that I would have preferred sleeping!

Governor Pataki had been introduced to Bear the "rescue dog" a week earlier at an ASPCA event on Pier 63. I'll never forget that night: I was the safety officer, and three people were seriously injured at different times during the evening. I had to rescue one and treat the other two in front of the Governor.

Later that morning, as I was preparing to check out of the hospital to go back to Ground Zero, I struck up a conversation with two survivors. In the course of hearing their emotionally-moving account of their escape and rescue I started to weep. A psychiatrist, complete with beard and pipe in hand, who was stationed at the hospital happened to observe me. He immediately called to a security officer and medical personnel for assistance. After a brief discussion that never included me, the psychiatrist and medical staff arranged for a police sergeant to have me transported back to Connecticut. They instructed me to go with this officer.

"Make sure he doesn't go back to the site," ordered the psychiatrist as they loaded Bear and me into the police van. Once again, I saw a decade of training go down the drain.

No sooner did we pull away from the hospital than the sergeant turned to me with a funny smile on his face. "Anywhere you want to go, Captain?" he asked.

Here was another hero. I grinned from ear to ear. "Take me back to the site, sergeant," I said. "We're not finished working yet."

III.

GOODWILL AMBASSADOR

"A dog has the soul of a philosopher."
Plato

Bear was the guest of honor at a memorial service in Manhattan at St. John the Divine Cathedral in September 2001. The Queen's Cold Stream Guard and 1st Battalion Scots Guard serenaded him. (British Army Photographer)

The 1st Battalion Scots Guard honored Bear on
four different occasions. This last time was in
Madison Square Park in NYC, in September
2002. Minutes after this photo was taken Bear was
rushed to the hospital. He never came home again.
(Nancy M. West)

The Scots Guard composed a "Lament for the
Golden Bear." Bear is now a little piece of British history.
(Arthur Freed)

POSTER DOG

The "human-canine bond" is frequently talked about in today's media. Bookshelves and magazine racks are full of stories about our relationships with our loyal companions, protectors, and co-workers. We're reminded that canines have stood by us in the best and the worst of times. It's no secret that the canines at Ground Zero not only led the rescuers in their difficult work but also brought comfort and relief to thousands on the site, and possibly millions around the world, as they worked alongside of us during our darkest of human hours. They symbolize the best of our efforts, and they let us know that as a species, we humans do not journey alone.

Bear's self-assuredness, composure, and accomplishments led him to become a kind of "poster dog" representing all of the search dogs at Ground Zero to the world. Because of Bear's inherent qualities, reporters and the general public alike wanted to see and hear more about him and his life. As time passed it became apparent to me and to others who knew us that Bear's popularity could be used to promote and achieve "good works" even after 9/11. To this end, Bear and I had the opportunity to publicize the need for medical insurance for all of the canines that worked at Ground Zero.

I brought Bear into this world under my office desk. Bear had always been a healthy dog; in fact, from the day he was born until 9/11, Bear had never been sick or injured a day in his life. Yet in the months after our time at Ground Zero, the puncture wound on his back that he had received at the site refused to heal and became cancerous, his weight dropped from 110 pounds to 85 pounds, and he developed muscle and nerve disorders. Bear's medical bills were mounting.

I was thrilled to receive word that a national pet insurance organization pledged that it would reimburse medical expenses for all canines that had worked the site. Grateful for this opportunity, I applied for assistance. Then I received a letter from the insurance company telling me that Bear wasn't covered because his neurological and skin cancer ailments "pre-dated" the offer for free insurance. I was shocked. Here was one more insurance company playing games with a precious life—this time, my dog's.

After nine months of his veterinary doctor submitting bills over and over again to the insurance company in an attempt to get coverage for Bear but meeting with no success, I contacted a friend in the media. It wasn't long before much of the world's major television and radio stations and newspapers were doing stories on Bear and the denial of coverage to some of the 9/11 rescue dogs. The controversy raged, and amid mounting public anger and adverse publicity, the insurance company president apologized on national television (CNN and FOX), saying the company had made an error. They then offered Bear lifetime coverage.

I refused the free lifetime insurance, explaining on CNN that this was not simply about Bear and me but about *all* of the search and rescue dog teams and their needs as well. I knew that Bear was famous now and he would be taken care of, but what about the others who had risked so much to serve the public good at the World Trade Center? Public pressure mounted, and the pet insurance company then publicly agreed to pay the medical bills for all of the dogs that had worked at Ground Zero—even if their medical claims pre-dated the offer for free insurance. However, between the time of the offer and the company's payment of three thousand dollars, Bear's medical bills jumped to over seven thousand dollars. The North Shore Animal League on Long Island stepped in and paid an additional three thousand dollars.

Ultimately Bear's total medical expenses climbed to over fifteen thousand dollars, yet as this book goes to print, a portion of Bear's medical bills *still* haven't been reimbursed to his veterinary doctor! What's even worse is that many of the almost 350 SAR canine teams were never contacted and made aware that an insurance reimbursement existed for their sick or injured dogs. I had to do something…but what?

THE BEAR SEARCH
AND RESCUE FOUNDATION

In the summer of 2002, the prestigious law firm of Proskauer & Rose helped to establish the Bear Search and Rescue Foundation. The mission of this foundation is threefold: to provide health care to all canines that worked at Ground Zero and at the Pentagon; to provide instruction in emergency management to search and rescue teams; and to equip these teams around the country.

Many of the search and rescue teams (both canine and non-canine) that train, equip, and answer the call for help around the world do so out of their own pockets. Even if they are part of a local, state, or federally-funded organization they might only obtain partial assistance for their expenses. Most SAR teams have local or state affiliations but still depend on donations to maintain their operations. These teams do not seek attention and public fanfare for their work, nor do they ask for monetary reimbursement. They do this job because *this is the work they love to do*. While much of their time involves answering requests to help find missing children or persons who have been kidnapped, they are always ready to answer calls for natural or man-made disasters—both here and abroad. These men, women, and canines complete their missions and quietly return home to their work-a-day lives until they are called to another natural or human-designed disaster. Often, as in the case at Ground Zero and Oklahoma City, these teams respond on a moment's notice. They drop whatever work or personal obligations they have and answer the call for help. Along with municipal police and fire personnel, they are often some of the very first rescuers on site to assist victims.

It is the mission of the Bear Search and Rescue Foundation to assist these individuals and groups. We have already provided rescue and management courses and much-needed equipment to urban search and rescue teams across the country, as well as individual SAR teams. Our mission is ongoing and we encourage search and rescue teams to contact us with their needs.

Furthermore, to remember many of these "unknown heroes," the Bear Search and Rescue Foundation now has presented awards to over a hundred men and women who had selflessly served their fellow citizens during some of our nation's darkest days at Ground Zero. The foundation is pledged to remember and honor these heroes in September of each year on board the USS Intrepid.

The foundation is also aided by Angel Flight, an organization of volunteer pilots that provide transport to people in need of specialized medical treatment to hospitals around the country. Angel Flight began transporting search and rescue teams to Ground Zero, and continues to transport such teams to areas where they are needed, in Bear's name. The foundation has close ties to Angel Flight, and a simple phone call can provide free air travel for search and rescue teams on a designated mission.

One of the greatest lessons to be gleaned from the World Trade Center tragedy may simply be *to be prepared should terrorism (or other disaster) strike again.* The Bear Search and Rescue Foundation hopes to add to this nationwide preparedness through supporting these devoted volunteer search and rescue teams, both canine and non-canine, across the country. We continue to uphold the motto, "So That Others May Live!"

SOME VERY SPECIAL HONORS

Since 9/11, Bear received many accolades from a myriad of organizations. Yet each time he received such honors I knew in my heart that it meant that *all* of the canines were really being remembered. Bear was honored in many ways, but there are several occasions that stand out in my mind.

For months after the World Trade Center tragedy I was overwhelmed by the extent of human loss I had seen. Friends who knew me well were concerned by my uncharacteristic somber mood. I never smiled or enjoyed a humorous moment. I wouldn't even indulge in a social drink. Like the military veterans returning from a war zone, many of us who had worked at Ground Zero were having trouble readjusting to our "civilian" lives. I received a call one day in early November from Roy Gross of the Suffolk County SPCA inviting Bear and me to the annual "International Cat Association Show" in White Plains, New York. They wished to give Bear a "Hero Dog of the Year" award. The irony of the "cats" honoring a dog…! This made me feel extremely proud, and it brought a smile to my face—my first since September 11th.

Earlier, in the fall of 2001, Bear and I were the honored guests at a memorial service at St. John the Divine, the largest Cathedral in the United States. Two of the Queen's House Guard Regiments, the Cold Stream Guard and the 1st Battalion Scots Guard, performed during the ceremony. These two regiments are not merely ceremonial. They're combat soldiers and have served in Great Britain's major conflicts around the world for over 300 years. It was a great honor when they serenaded Bear.

Amazingly, over the course of the following year, the Scots Guard honored Bear on four other occasions. The last time while he was alive was in Madison Square Park in September of 2002. At the time Bear had been ill, and we were waiting for his blood test results. Yet it was a beautiful day, and I knew that the British soldiers wanted to see him one more time. At the end of their public performance, Pipe Major Paul Selwood announced that they would play a tribute to Bear, a song they normally play when marching back to work at Buckingham Palace. He said it was "spookily called 'The Black Bear'." What Pipe Major Selwood didn't know was that only moments before his announcement, I had received a phone call from Dr. Chaitman telling me that Bear's blood test results were dangerously "off the charts," and that he needed to be rushed to the hospital immediately. While the pipes wailed I could feel the tears welling up in my eyes. Then I was asked to say a few words. I gave a short speech on how there was *hope for humanity* because 300 years ago the ancestors of the Scots' Guard were chasing our ancestors through the fields of Long Island, across Long Island Sound, and into the hills of Connecticut. And now, all these years later, our bitter enemy has become our best friend and closest ally.

Since then I have often reflected on how appropriate it was that the first group to honor Bear was also the last. We went from the park directly to the hospital, and Bear never came home again.

Several months later Heather Bain, Director of the American-Scottish Foundation, contacted me to say she had a package for me from the Scots Guard, and would like to have a little ceremony to present it. A meeting was arranged with Heather at the Society of Illustrators in New York, where Bear also had been honored on several occasions. When Heather handed me a framed sheet of martial music written by Pipe Lance Sergeant Lowther of the Guard entitled, "Lament for the Golden Bear," tears rolled down my cheeks. There was now British martial music written into history forever for my boy.

But Bear also received other awards before his death. I was touched by history when Chet Marcus, a friend and an Army Public Affairs Officer in New York, requested our presence at the annual memorial to the "Lost Battalion" in Central Park. This ceremony honors the outnumbered and surrounded lost battalion of the 77th "Liberty Division" in the Argonne forest in France during the First World War. The men were cut-off and surrounded for six days without shelter, food, and a supply of water, but they held the enemy off and became the stuff of legends. Only 200 of the 600 men survived. On the south side of the band shell in the park is a field with stones inscribed to honor members of the Lost Battalion. Although I had considered not attending (I had been to so many ceremonies honoring departed friends that sadness was overwhelming me), I had read a lot about these brave soldiers of legendary stature over my lifetime and, once asked to join these honors, wished to salute their memory.

When I arrived I was surprised to be asked to stand next to the French Ambassador. After the Ambassador received an award on behalf of the Army for the great friendship and alliance between his country and ours, General Colt of the 77th Regional Support Command called Bear (and me) to the podium. I was astounded when he presented us with the Commanding General's *Award for Outstanding Performance*. Chet Marcus had never told me that Bear and I were to be a part of the program when he invited us. I was most honored to have this award presented to me by General Colt because not only is he a soldier I have always admired, but he's a great leader who always puts the welfare of his troops first.

In the months after 9/11, Bear and I were also invited to visit many schools in the greater New York area. One of these was my alma mater P.S. 183 in Manhattan. My family moved to Manhattan from Miami when I was ten years old, and I have very fond memories of these years at this warm and cheerful grammar school. The day

Bear and I went to meet the kids and give our little presentation, the principal, Eric Byrne, surprised me with a fact I had long forgotten. Speaking to the audience he said that they had looked up my records and discovered that, way back when, I had been captain of the school safety patrol. Giving me a sly grin he added, "And he's *still* captain of the safety patrol!"

Several months later I received the school's yearbook in the mail. Bear's picture, holding a P.S. 183 hat in his mouth, was repeated in rows up and down the cover. Inside the book's cover was a photograph taken at the school with the following written by the school's reporters, Samantha Stone and Maya Kurien:

"Hero definition: One That Shows Great Courage. At 10:00 on September 11th the kids at P.S. 183 were unaware of what danger took place that morning. Throughout the day, parents rushed from work to pick up their kids. "Mommy, what happened?" "Dad, I was in the middle of Free Time," were some of the things parents of New York (and everywhere else) heard. Some parents all around New York were too afraid to tell their children the truth. September 11th was a shock to everybody. Although most of us didn't know about the horror, one team did.

When Bear's owner, Captain Scott Shields (former student of P.S.183!) heard, the amazing duo immediately rushed to the scene. Shields and his dog Bear risked their own lives to try to save the lives of others. Therefore, they are real heroes of New York. We never noticed that before the attack. We stood in line for hours to get our favorite movie star's autograph, but now we wait to get autographs of from EMS workers, firemen, and other heroes of New York. A few months later Captain Shields and his gifted dog came to our school. We were so thankful we were speechless. He answered all of our questions and explained what happened. We were so amazed that a real hero was a graduate of our school. We guess that means when we grow up we can all be heroes too."

Reading the words of the children and seeing Bear on the cover of the yearbook meant more to me than any other award we received…before or since.

Bear is probably one of the very few if not the only canine ever to receive two different state senate proclamations giving him his own special day of commemoration. In the fall of 2002, shortly after Bear's death, the New York State Senate proclaimed October 13, 2002, "Captain Shields and Bear Day in New York State." It was a tremendous honor. Then, in the spring of 2003 I received a phone call from Connecticut Senator Judith Freedman's office telling me that the State Senate and Governor Rowland would like to honor Bear and me with an award. Naturally I was honored to say "yes." They called me back several weeks later and asked when my birthday would be. I responded July 9th, and they scheduled the ceremony for that day. It was a very emotional day for me. Together with Senator Freedman, various state officials, family, and friends we gathered at Sherwood Island State Park in Westport, Connecticut at the site of the Ground Zero Memorial. This simple stone block memorial sits on a peaceful promontory overlooking Long Island Sound, and is dedicated to those who lost their lives at the World Trade Center. This particular location was selected for the memorial because local citizens gathered at this promontory on September 11th, and prayed for their friends and loved ones who were in harm's way that fateful day. From this vantage point they could see the insidious black smoke rising from lower Manhattan into the clear blue sky. Governor Rowland's office, the Connecticut State Assembly, and the State Senate all separately issued proclamations making July 9th, 2003, "Captain Shields and Bear Day in Connecticut." Not only was I honored to receive these awards in this hallowed spot, I was also deeply moved to receive these honors in Westport, the town where Bear had been born and raised. I also found it fitting that Senator Freedman bestowed some of the awards. She has always been a great proponent for open spaces, and it was these open parks and woodlands in and around Westport that allowed Bear to grow and develop into the dog he became. This was also the only ceremony my mother, Susan Shields, has been well enough to attend, so it held an extra special meaning for me. And I know that it meant the world to her to see her son honored in her home state of Connecticut.

SAYING GOODBYE

During the months after our work at Ground Zero Bear's health rapidly deteriorated. Not only did his weight plummet, but his agility decreased dramatically. He could no longer jump through the window of my car and his legs began to collapse under him unexpectedly when he was taking an easy stroll down the street. Many tests were performed but the extent of his illness remained a mystery until he was operated on for what we all thought was acute pancreatitis. When Bear was operated on at the Animal Medical Center in Manhattan, his surgeon discovered that he had a half a dozen different kinds of cancers.

Bear never recovered from this surgery. Three days later I was at home when the hospital called to say that Bear had gone into cardiac arrest. I knew that Bear would die and I was terrified that he would die without me being with him. Unlike Bear's local vet hospital (Veterinary Internal Medicine and Allergy Specialists of New York) where I could be with him 24/7, the Animal Medical Center could not let me stay with him. The thought of Bear being kept in a cage, something that he had never been in, broke my heart. I jumped in a taxi, hoping that one of my two wishes would be granted. I wanted to be with Bear when he died. My other hope was that I could bury him as a fireman, for to me, after 9/11 there can be no greater honor.

When I arrived at the hospital he was in the emergency room hooked up to intravenous solutions and a heart monitor. They brought him back countless times so that I could be with him at the end and have a little more time with him. Finally they said he couldn't be brought back again and still be himself. I said, "Okay then, it's time." It was the one decision in life I never wanted to have to make.

One of the doctors took out a candy-pink-colored vial of liquid and attached it to his intravenous tube. They said Bear would just go to sleep, but he didn't. As Bear had struggled so bravely in life, he struggled against death, a fighter to the bitter end.

Bear finally closed his eyes and died in my arms at 6:47 PM on September 23, 2002. Along with the day his mom, Honey, died, it was the saddest day of my life.

A FIREMAN'S FAREWELL

My second wish was granted: Bear was given a fireman's farewell. The Animal Medical Center staff lined the street outside the hospital to honor Bear as his remains were carried out in a plain cardboard box. The hospital staff had been wonderful to us and I will always remember their kindness. Bear was taken by a convoy of trucks from the NY Aviation Volunteer Fire Department, Engine Company 3, to the Hartsdale Pet Cemetery in Hartsdale, New York. Bear was cremated there. Today, his ashes sit in a simple brass urn in a special spot in my home. The inscription reads: "Bear: Hero of the World Trade Center."

On October 27th 2002, Bear's memorial service was held on the aircraft carrier USS Intrepid in New York. Angel Flight, the organization of volunteer pilots that provided transportation to search and rescue teams and brought in supplies for the canines from across the country during the 9/11 crisis, performed a missing man formation in Bear's honor. As taps were being played I looked out across the hundreds of mourners in attendance and I couldn't help but think that this tribute was not for Bear alone. It was for all the dogs and all the human heroes who had worked so tirelessly and bravely. I had also arranged in advance that this would be a tribute to all of us, and not just for Bear. To this end, the Bear Search and Rescue Foundation honored a hundred others at his memorial service. In retrospect, I like to say that Bear was just a dog, but by this I mean that he was imbued with the best of what we might call our humanity.

The first annual Bear Search and Rescue Foundation
ceremony aboard the USS Intrepid. We were able to
honor over 100 heroes of 9/11 that day.
(David Mintzer)

Bear going on his last journey. He received a fireman's send-off.
I can think of no greater honor for man or canine.
(Nancy M. West)

WHAT THE DOGS CAN TELL US

As a result of my training in national disaster management and because of what I knew from conversations with HazMat specialists, I requested that samples of Bear's tissue be sent to the Department of Agriculture after his death. I happened to know from other work I have done that they have one of the best HazMat labs in the world. I also requested that samples be sent to the military for analysis. My feeling was that the rescue dogs' medical problems that arose from working at Ground Zero would be the precursor of possible illnesses humans might face from having lived and worked in what we darkly called the "toxic soup" at Ground Zero. A few hours after my request Bear's surgeon informed me that samples would be sent to a medical center where a private organization was collecting data on the World Trade Center dogs that had died. My response was, "Great! The more labs doing analysis, the better." With three separate groups collecting data I saw this as the best way to maximize the ability to get to the truth.

"Sorry," the surgeon responded, "We've been told that if we send Bear's samples to any other organization he'll be thrown out of the private research study." I was stunned. It was difficult enough to think of my "little man" being dead, but then to be told that his tissue was subject to an academic turf war, or something even more sinister, upset me greatly. I was so emotionally distraught at his death that I agreed to let them send his tissue samples to the private group.

In an article published in the July 26, 2003, issue of the *Denver Post*, reporter Diedtra Henderson writes that the private research study is closely following 97 canines from Ground Zero and the

Pentagon over a three-year period. The article quotes this research group as stating that *the three-year study will be a too-brief snapshot to capture many medical woes.* At this writing it's my knowledge that only a dozen police dogs from Ground Zero and the Pentagon are being watched on an ongoing basis by a different organization to see if they develop specific toxin-related illnesses. Considering that nearly 350 canines worked at Ground Zero and the Pentagon, and that there were different toxins present at the two sites, this does not seem prudent or logical.

Yet part of the problem stems from the fact that no one ever kept track of all of the dogs at Ground Zero! Once these canine teams went home many were not communicated with again. This is different from the situation at the Oklahoma City bombing, where all 74 of the dogs that worked at the site were tracked and studied for illnesses and injuries. This comprehensive study was undertaken and completed by The Department of Agriculture and printed in the *Journal of the Veterinary Medical Association.* Because of the enormous devastation at Ground Zero and the potentiality of long-term health effects to humans, we can only hope that this private study will be expanded, or a comprehensive, government-backed study will be undertaken, and more data from the dogs included. Forewarned is forearmed, and these dogs, many of whom have died, could hold the key to any health problems that humans who worked on the pile might face in the future. In my opinion cancer (which Bear had several times over) and other illnesses could eventually arise in the rescue workers.

In the spring of 2003, the Environmental Protection Agency's (EPA) Office of the Inspector General issued a report concluding that the agency had released an inaccurate preliminary report about the air quality at Ground Zero. In an article published in the March 16, 2003, issue of the *Sacramento Bee*, reporters Chris Bowman and Edie Lau quote the report as follows:

"The EPA did not have sufficient data to declare the ambient air 'safe to breath' when it did.... The EPA had data on only four of fourteen pollutants that scientists believe the public potentially was exposed to immediately after the collapse of the twin towers.... Also, the inspection team said it learned that the EPA applied a dramatically higher level of 'accepted risk' in making its pronouncements.... The EPA reached its conclusion using a cancer risk level 100 times greater than what it traditionally deems acceptable for public exposure to toxic air contaminants."

All of this again points to the fact that studying the fate of the SAR canines is vitally important to all of us.

THEODORE(ABLE)

In the weeks after Bear died I hardly wanted to get up in the morning. My friends were growing concerned, yet having been with Bear 24/7 for nearly thirteen years, I was lost without him. One day my friend Dawn Wladyka, who has a wonderful golden named Virgil, phoned to say that she and a few other friends of mine thought that it was time for me to be a "dad" again. Theodore, a.k.a. "Theodore(able)," entered my life, and is rapidly stealing my heart. He resembles Bear in size (both height and brawn), has reddish-brown fur, and has a profile that is the spitting image of Bear's. At times, the resemblance is uncanny. People who are not aware that Bear is dead often stop me on the street and mistake Theodore for Bear.

At this writing, Theodore is currently hard at work in search and rescue training. His "finds" were mostly lost gloves and dollar bills until recently. We were called on a mission with the NYC Urban Parks Search and Rescue team to look for a kidnapped adult. Although we didn't locate the missing person, Theodore discovered the hideout for several vagrants who had been conducting petty thefts in a Bronx neighborhood. Theodore tracked two miles down a riverbed, through a swamp, and up a fifty-foot bridge abutment to find the hideout.

Through Theodore and the Bear Search and Rescue Foundation it is my hope that Bear's good work will continue, and that the memory of all the canine and human heroes who responded to the "911" call will never be forgotten and will continue to be supported "so that others may live."

Theodore and I at the Owego, New York, airport.
Theodore(able), as I like to call him, is quickly
stealing my heart and living up to Bear's standards
(Donna Easton)

DREAMS

To this day I dream about Honey and Bear often. Sometimes these dreams take the shape of nightmares. I had one recently where I lost Honey in a landslide. Bear and I searched and searched, but we could never find her. It was a horrible dream, and I woke up in a sweat. Other times, though, these dreams take me back to our carefree lives before Ground Zero. Sometimes I dream that Honey and Bear and I are wading through piles of autumn leaves or running through the shallows at Compo Beach in Westport. They run to the shore and roll over for me to give them belly rubs. Often, Bear and Honey and I are out on my boat enjoying the day, exploring the vast beaches and marshes along the Connecticut shoreline. We anchor the boat and jump in for a swim. It's a day filled with endless possibilities.

APPENDIX

Dr. Jane Goodall, DBE, UN Messenger of Peace, Founder, Jane Goodall Institute, and Scott Shields, President, The Bear Search and Rescue Foundation. Taken at the foundation's Fourth Annual Extraordinary Service to Humanity Awards ceremony at the USS Intrepid Sea-Air-Space Museum in New York City. (Michael Gromet)

SCOTT'S POEMS

"My Brothers"

i met my brothers
The other day
Again
Though they were not born of my mother
They will always be my brothers,
Though i may never see them again
They will always be my brothers,

For we outlived that day
And walked out of hell
Late one September night
T.J., Jon-Paul, Bear, and me,

"Bear did his job better than any
dog that followed
Better than any dog ever did,"
Jon-Paul said.

Ask any fireman who led us!
One Golden Man

T.J. believed in him
And stayed after others moved on,
And my young brother Jon-Paul
Crawled into the void
Found Chief Ganci
And suffers to this day,

And Bear, and T.J., and Jon-Paul and i
All we did was our job
And we would do it all again
Despite the toll

And the woman said,
"Get that dog on a leash
and off the memorial!"

and i yelled

"He led us all
He's got as much right
to stand here
as any man who served."

And the man from the history channel got it all on tape.

-By Captain Scott Shields

The Years of Bear

They came to get Bear today
and what do you say
about a "Hero"
that is your son
and may have died
because you took him for a walk
in hell

The Fire Engine came
and they placed his remains
lovingly, inside
 Fire Engines and Firemen
will never mean the same thing
 they did before that
warm september day

what conversation
do you have with yourself
about the guilt you feel
about that one more year
He might have lived
if you and He had not done your duty

How fitting for a Hero of the
World Trade Center
To be cremated

Should you have worried more
about you and yours
instead of, them and their's

If the truth be known
maybe
but you and he never would have thought of
yourselves first
it was not in his nature
or yours

Remember how he would protect
a little dog against
a big one?

or let any girl dog bite him
or never start a fight
or how he never lost one

except the one no one
can ever win
and even then how he fought against
the darkness

even knowing what I know now
we would have walked
straight into hell
together

my friend Arthur Freed said
"Chief Peter Ganci and Father Judge
must have told God
that the thousands
who perished on that September day
could use a Great dog
to comfort them.........
I shall never stroke a golden coat
again
without thinking of Bear

Thank you, and Honey
for giving us all
The Years of Bear

LETTERS AND AWARDS

- United Nations, 2003 World Peace Month, ("As an Example of a Hero to Humanity")
- New York State Senate (Hero Proclamation – October 13, 2002 Declared Captain Shields and Bear Day in State of New York)
- New Jersey General Assembly (Hero Proclamation – September 21, 2003)
- Connecticut General Assembly (Hero Proclamation – July 9, 2003 Declared Captain Shields and Bear Day in State of Connecticut)
- New York Columbus Day Parade 2001 (Marched at head of Parade)
- 1st Battalion Scots Guards (honored numerous times)
- Guiding Eyes for the Blind (Hero Award)
- Emergency Response Division, New York Sanitation Dept. (For Extraordinary Service)
- New York Illustrator's Society (Painting by award winning canine illustrator 2001 Steve Parton) "Prevailing Human Spirit" Tour
- Broadway Barks (Outstanding Service Award Presented By Bernadette Peters and Mary Tyler Moore)
- International Cat Association (Hero Dog of the Year 2001)
- The Human Society of New York (Outstanding Efforts in Rescue and Relief)
- Norwalk Seaport (Outstanding Service to Humanity Award presented by Connecticut 's Governor Rowland)
- US Army 77th Division Regional Support Command (Commanding General's Award for Outstanding Performance)
- USS Intrepid (Honored for Heroism)
- New York City Urban Parks Department (Made First Canine Member)
- American Cancer Society (Canine Hero Award)
- Lindbergh Foundation (Spirit of St. Louis Medal)
- Nancy Gellman Award (Service to Humanity)
- Leukemia and Lymphoma Society (Canine Hero Award)

this

"*Heroes' Award*"

is presented to

Bear, the Rescue Dog,
and Scott Shields, Handler

by the Westchester Cat Show

in recognition of
your invaluable contribution
to the rescue effort at the
World Trade Center Disaster Site.

November 17, 2001

SOCIETY OF ILLUSTRATORS

THE SOCIETY OF ILLUSTRATORS

RECOGNIZES THE EXTRAORDINARY EFFORT

AND UNIQUE TALENT OF

BEAR

IN HIS ROLE AS RESCUE DOG ON

9/11/01

In documentation of
testimonials to "Bear"
in conjunction with the exhibition
Prevailing Human Spirit

January 10, 2002
and
September 11, 2002

President, Society of Illustrators

United States Army

77th Regional Support Command

CERTIFICATE OF ACHIEVEMENT

is awarded to

Capt. Scott Shields and Bear

For meritorious service to the citizens of New York

From September 11, 2001 to September 10, 2002

Richard S. Colt
Major General, USAR
Commanding

Date

77TH RSC Form 39
Sept 99

SENATOR THOMAS W. LIBOUS

Proclamation

Honoring

Captain Scott Shields

A True Hero from Ground Zero

Whereas, Within every community there exist certain individuals who, through their hard work, dedication and service, play an instrumental role in protecting the lives of its citizens; and

Whereas, One such individual is Captain Scott Shields, along with the beloved late "Bear," who are being honored today for their heroic efforts in the search and rescue mission at Ground Zero on and after September 11, 2001; and

Whereas, Captain Scott Shields, one of the first rescuers to respond after the attacks, used his extensive background in emergency management to organize harbor activities, utilizing boats for rescue and emergency transportation efforts and communicating with other crafts for assistance; and

Whereas, Captain Scott Shields and his companion "Bear" were the first canine team to arrive at Ground Zero, working tirelessly in the search and rescue mission, locating the body of the beloved FDNY Chief Peter J. Ganci, Jr., and remaining at Ground Zero for six months assisting with the recovery efforts; and

Whereas, Captain Scott Shields has displayed the human values of bravery and dedication as a member of the firefighting community, achieving success that is shared by his family, many friends and colleagues; now therefore be it

Resolved, That Sunday, October 13, 2002 be proclaimed "Captain Scott Shields Day" in the 51st New York State Senate District; and be it further

Resolved, That a copy of this Proclamation, suitably engrossed, be presented to Captain Scott Shields, as an expression of the high esteem in which he is held by his fellow citizens of this Empire State.

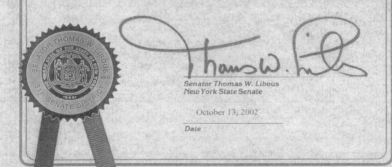

Senator Thomas W. Libous
New York State Senate

October 13, 2002

Date

State of Connecticut

By His Excellency JOHN G. ROWLAND, Governor: an

Official Statement

Today, the State of Connecticut honors the memory
and the heroic efforts of

Bear.

In the delicate balance of life, cries were heard from the New York harbor—to the fields of Pennsylvania—to the heart of our Nation's Capitol. The visible horror of the Twin Towers collapsing, the thick, black smoke and heavy debris sweeping through the avenues and streets, and our neighbors, friends and loved ones running in fear and uncertainty searching for safety, discolored our comprehension and exposed our vulnerability.

Through the confusion and chaos, ordinary citizens, like Scott Shields and his rescue canine, Bear, became heroes answering the urgent call to humanity. In those most difficult times, the spirit of America rose through our pain and sorrow. The spirit was in the hearts and the minds of all citizens, the rescue workers, the medical personnel, the firefighters, the policemen, the search and rescue canines and their handlers, and those who gave blood. It was the true strength of the human race. In our darkest hour, we held firmly to our values and basic principles allowing hope, faith, pride and courage to lead our Nation and the State of Connecticut.

Scott Shields and Bear bravely demonstrated a tremendous amount of strength, a kind heart, a quick mind, and a calm composure while giving tirelessly of their talents to aid those in most need. I salute their dedication and ultimate sacrifice. Due in part to their heroism, Connecticut is a stronger community dedicated to the qualities of kindness, compassion, and love.

Therefore, I, JOHN G. ROWLAND, Governor of the State of Connecticut, in recognition of their dedicated efforts in response to September 11th, do hereby proclaim July 9, 2003 as

SCOTT SHIELDS AND BEAR DAY

in the State of Connecticut. I urge all our citizens to join me in thanking Scott Shields and Bear for their tireless and unselfish contributions of time, energy, talents and expertise.

John G. Rowland
Governor

State of Connecticut

QUI TRANSTULIT SUSTINET

General Assembly

In emoriam

Be it hereby known to all that:
The Connecticut General Assembly
extends its sincerest condolences
and expressions of sympathy to:

CAPTAIN SCOTT SHIELDS

on the passing of

"BEAR" THE DOG. "BEAR" WAS A TRUE HERO WHO WILL BE FOREVER REMEMBERED AS THE DOG WHO SAVED LIVES IN THE AFTERMATH OF SEPTEMBER 11, 2001.

Introduced by Senator Judith G. Freedman of the 26th District
Representative Cathy Tymniak of the 133rd District
Representative G. Kenneth Bernhard of the 136th District

Given this 11th day of November 20 02

President Pro Tempore

Speaker of the House

Secretary of the State

New Jersey
General Assembly
Washington

Citation

Commendations and praise are extended to

CAPTAIN SCOTT SHIELDS & BEAR

by the citizenry of the 29th New Jersey Legislative District, through their elected representative,

Assemblyman Wilfredo Caraballo

For their courageous acts of heroism, given beyond measure and without regard for personal safety, in which they demonstrated an exemplary and uncommon concern for the lives of others.

September 21, 2003
Date

Wilfredo Caraballo,
Member of the General Assembly

The Humane Society of New York

Gratefully Acknowledges
Captain Scott Shields and Bear

for

Outstanding Efforts in the Rescue and Relief Mission

of the

September 11th Disaster

President

GUIDING EYES FOR THE BLIND

611 GRANITE SPRINGS ROAD
YORKTOWN HEIGHTS, NEW YORK 10598

was pleased to be joined by

HERO DOG BEAR

a Golden Retriever credited with finding and saving the most people on September 11, 2001 and following

and by

CAPT. SCOTT SHIELDS

Marine Safety Service

at

Ben Benson's Steak House
123 W. 52nd Street
New York City

On June 1, 2002

Certificate of Recognition

In recognition of your outstanding service to the community
and with grateful appreciation
for the many ways you enrich the lives of those whose paths you cross,
Broadway Barks presents this certificate of merit to

BEAR

on this 13th day of July, 2002.

Bernadette Peters
Bernadette Peters

Mary Tyler Moore
Mary Tyler Moore

...d to Captain Shields Bear, Virgil, and Theodore

A Pledge of Gratitude

...tude is dedicated to our heroes and friends in every Fire Department Police ...nd Emergency Medical Service Unit in America especially those who have ...suffered personal loss during the tragedies on September 11 2001

...a beacon of light. Like the stars stitched onto our flag, you guide us towards ...our darkest hours. You extend your powerful hands to us, gently, no matter ...ar you must reach. We depend on you, clinging to the safety in your eyes. When ...become lost in the empty caverns of despair, you remind us to climb out and salvage ...very last piece of our indestructible American spirit. You inspire us to fight for life, to hold on. In our search for humanity, we saw tears cutting rivers through the dust on your cheeks. Not one of those tears fell alone. In our search for strength, we witnessed your sacrifices, given without hesitation, and the losses are too much to bear.

Heroes are not mythological creatures, not comic book legends or Hollywood icons. Real heroes are human (and, in some cases, animal). They bleed. They cry. They save. You reflect the essence of true heroism. Yet, when you are described as heroic, you wince as though "hero" is a title too grand. Quite the contrary, the word is too small to describe what you do. You run directly into nightmares to protect us. Sentinels of our nation, you defy the face of terror. When you leave for work, do you kiss your family goodbye and secretly pray it will not be the last? Do you wonder if today will test the limits of your bravery? In spite of the fears that must crouch in the shadows of your mind, you depart for work each day with a commitment to help others. You push exhaustion aside, bear the grief of fallen comrades. It is unthinkable that we sometimes forget to thank you. We forget to smile or wave, even mumble a simple "hello." Please know that only our voices have failed you. Our hearts cry out, even when our words don't, "Thank you! Thank you!" That phrase is whispered in our dreams at night, repeated in the moments of peace you fought for us to have.

We hereby pledge our profound appreciation for all you have sacrificed in the name of our safety. We pay tribute to you for the selflessness you demonstrate each day. We honor you for your bravery, your humanity, and your drive to keep helping even while your souls ache. Inspired by your courage, we will fight to survive, hold up our heads, and be proud of our country's resilience. Thank you for being the heroes of our United States. Words cannot fully express the depths of our gratitude and so, we salute you. May you be blessed and protected now, tomorrow, and always.

With love, gratitude, and respect,

Your friends at White Plains High School

ARTHUR FREED, P.E., F.NSPE
6 Patricia Lane
White Plains, New York 10605-4009
Consulting Engineers

September 27, 2002

Capt. Scott Shields
225 Rector Place
New York, NY 10280

Dear Scott:

Judy and I were deeply saddened to learn of the passing of our beloved friend Bear.

Our weekend trips to the Battery were always accompanied by the anticipation that we might meet Bear. When we did, and I was able to pet him, it was a special event and a happier day.

Peter Ganci and Father Judge must have told God that the thousands who perished on September 11th could use a great dog to comfort them. What better dog could God have chosen? While that is now Bear's greater calling, his memory lives on with the drowning child whose life he saved, the work he did at Ground Zero, the Columbus Day parade he led, and the countless times he was the center of attention at events throughout the tri-state area. How wonderful you should feel having lovingly cared for him all these years, and thus enabled those things to happen.

I shall never stroke a golden coat again without thinking of Bear. Of course you are still welcome to our home, and we hope you will call us when you find the time to come. Thank you for giving us all the years of Bear, and the greater good he now is doing.

Sincerely,

ARTHUR FREED, P.E., F.NSPE

White Plains, New York • Bedford, Massachusetts

Phone: (914) 997-7068   Fax: (914) 997-7068   E-Mail: jdyfreed@earthlink.net

ʃ THE AUTHORS

Photo—Nancy West

Captain Scott Shields is the former Director of Marine Safety for the New York City Urban Parks Search and Rescue Team. He is a graduate of the National Inter-agency Civil Military Institute, based in California (Military Assistance to Civil Authority), and holds certifications from FEMA and the Red Cross. Captain Shields lives in New York City with his dog "Theodore." Captain Shields was Bear's dad.

Photo—Lynda Shenkman Curtis

Nancy M. West is the author of *Chips: The War Dog,* a novel for children based on the most-decorated canine from the Second World War. She is currently at work on a new book about the lives of search and rescue dogs and their handlers.